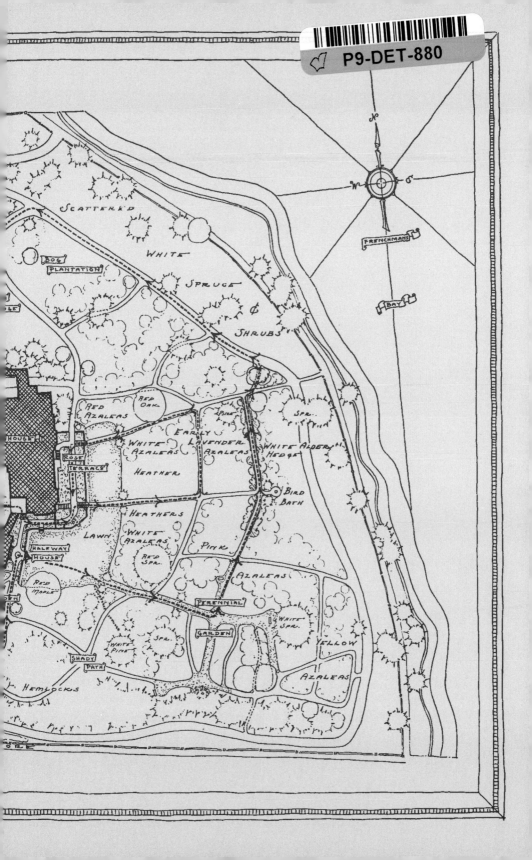

The Bulletins of

REEF POINT GARDENS

Beatrix Farrand

BEATRIX FARRAND

The Bulletins of
REEF POINT GARDENS

Introduction by Paula Deitz

Paula Deitz

THE ISLAND FOUNDATION
Bar Harbor, Maine

Distributed by Sagapress, Inc.

Publication of
The Bulletins of Reef Point Gardens
is a project of The Island Foundation,
and the proceeds from its sale will go toward
establishing an endowment for the
Asticou Azalea Garden
in Northeast Harbor, Maine.

Edited and indexed by Carol Betsch
Design and composition by Dale Swensson
Production coordinated by Anthony Richmond

LIBRARY OF CONGRESS CATALOGING-IN-PUBLICATION DATA
Reef Point Gardens bulletin.
The bulletins of Reef Point Gardens / Beatrix Farrand :
introduction by Paula Deitz.
p. cm.
Facsimile reprints of the 17 Reef Point Gardens bulletins,
written by Beatrix Farrand and others,
and published 1946–1956.
Includes index.
ISBN 0-89831-052-0 (hardcover)
1. Reef Point Gardens (Bar Harbor, Me.) 2. Farrand, Beatrix, 1872–1959—
Homes and haunts—Maine—Bar Harbor.
I. Farrand, Beatrix, 1872–1959. II. Title.
SB466.U7R44 1997
635'.09741'45—dc21 97-6726

Printed in the United States of America

In memory of

PEGGY ROCKEFELLER

whose years of loving care

enhanced the beauty of

a great Beatrix Farrand garden

CONTENTS

Foreword

In 1946, Beatrix Farrand wrote the first *Reef Point Gardens Bulletin.* Fifteen more were published in the next ten years until, in 1956, the gardens ceased to exist. Mrs. Farrand wrote the last Bulletin after she realized that she could no longer find support for Reef Point and had the house torn down. On the dissolution of Reef Point, the property was purchased by the architect Robert W. Patterson, Vice President of the Reef Point Gardens Corporation and a long-time friend and associate of Mrs. Farrand.

In order to save the extraordinary collection of plants remaining in the gardens—a collection considered to be the finest north of the Arnold Arboretum in Jamaica Plain, Massachusetts—Charles K. Savage, another member of the corporation, proposed the creation of two gardens in Northeast Harbor: the Thuya Garden, on the hill above the Asticou Terraces, and the Asticou Azalea Garden, across the road from the Asticou Inn. The purchase of Mrs. Farrand's plants and the design of these two gardens by Charles Savage was accomplished with the financial support of John D. Rockefeller, Jr., another friend of Beatrix Farrand. Beginning in 1926, Mrs. Farrand had designed the Eyrie Garden in Seal Harbor for Mr. Rockefeller and his wife, Abby Aldrich Rockefeller.

The Asticou Azalea Garden was planted first, while the site of the Thuya Garden was used as a holding area for Mrs. Farrand's collections. Charles Savage was a man of exceptional talents: from an alder swamp he created a Japanese stroll garden of great beauty, where the ponds reflect the azaleas and rhododendrons from Reef Point.

These Bulletins are being reprinted by the Asticou Azalea Garden Committee of The Island Foundation. In addition to representing a document of interest to the horticulturist and the historian of American gardens, they tell an intimate story of a beloved place and of the courage with which its loss was met, which is so revealing of the character of Beatrix Farrand.

Now owned and maintained by The Island Foundation, the Asticou Azalea Garden provides the setting where Beatrix Farrand's plants, since grown to maturity, continue to flourish as a living memorial to the great gardener who collected them.

BETH STRAUS, *Chairman*
Asticou Azalea Garden Committee

"Open to All Real Plant Lovers": Beatrix Farrand's Invitation to Reef Point Gardens

Written words and illustrations outlive many plantations." This was Beatrix Farrand's farsighted view in 1955 when she acknowledged that her cherished gardens at Reef Point could no longer be maintained to her satisfaction. *The Bulletins of Reef Point Gardens* essentially bears out the truth of that statement. Written by Mrs. Farrand and her colleagues over a period of ten years, these Bulletins preserve what she referred to finally as the less important "out-of-door phase" of her gardens. One of the premier landscape gardeners of the twentieth century, Beatrix Farrand (1872–1959) created at Reef Point, her family's summer residence, a private showcase of native and naturalized plantings that evolved into the only botanic garden then in the state of Maine.

The idea for the Reef Point Gardens Bulletins originated with her husband, Max Farrand, a distinguished author and professor of Constitutional history. With his "disciplined scholar's mind," wrote Beatrix Farrand, he "felt that publication was an essential part of the gardens' work." Prior to his death in 1945, he even suggested a list of topics and approved a selection of material submitted, and the Max Farrand Memorial Fund became the official publisher of the Bulletins. Along with Reef Point's extensive horticultural library, documents collection and herbarium, the Bulletins became an equal partner in the Gardens' mission. Distributed to botanic gardens, arboreta and libraries worldwide and sold to local visitors for ten cents a copy, they were shaped over the years to contain the essence of the entire landscape. At the time of their publication, everyone associated with Reef Point Gardens had high hopes for its future as a public garden and educational center, organized specifically to expose students of landscape architecture to horticultural expertise and design. Now these Bulletins, published here for the first time in facsimile form along with supplementary material about Mrs. Farrand and her gardens, are what remain of a horticultural adventure that came to an end in 1955.

In addition to the landscape gardener herself, four other writers are represented in this collection. Amy Magdalene Garland (1899–1996), who became the chief horticulturist of Reef Point, was born in Bishop's Waltham in Hampshire, England. She arrived in New York City just after World War I to work for Mrs. Farrand's mother, Mary Cadwalader Jones, as a domestic in her Greenwich Village house. In time, she married Lewis A. Garland, the handyman and chauffeur at Reef Point, and developed into a trusted collaborator in maintaining and documenting the plant collection.

Robert Whiteley Patterson (1905–1988), a 1927 graduate of Harvard College, returned to the university in 1932 to study landscape architecture at the Graduate School of

Design. He first went to Maine in 1934 as a designer and planner for Acadia National Park and met Beatrix Farrand at that time. Later, he maintained an office at Reef Point as her associate.

Marion Ida Spaulding (1908–1994) was a landscape architect who completed her degree at the Rhode Island School of Design in 1947. She worked at Reef Point for long periods between 1946 and 1952 to create the herbarium and map the gardens into sections for record-keeping purposes. Later, settling in New Hampshire, she became the resident designer at Mt. Gunstock Nursery in Gilford and was also associated with the Laconia Housing and Redevelopment Authority.

And finally, Kenneth A. Beckett (b. 1929), a young Englishman, spent six months as a skilled gardener and propagator at Reef Point in 1954 after receiving his Royal Horticultural Society Diploma from the Wisley School of Horticulture. He eventually became a prominent garden writer in Britain, and among his more than forty publications is the popular *Royal Horticultural Society Encylopaedia of House and Conservatory Plants*. Now living in Norfolk, he looks back on the two Bulletins he wrote for Mrs. Farrand as his first ambitious work.

Although the name Reef Point visually connotes an isolated property projecting out into one of the myriad bays along the rugged coast of Maine, the original two-acre plot purchased in 1882 by Frederic Rhinelander Jones, Beatrix's father, was actually located in the middle of Bar Harbor, the then newly fashionable summer community on Mount Desert Island. Expanded by later purchases to six acres, Reef Point lies between Hancock Street and Atlantic Avenue, two side streets that run perpendicular to the Shore Path. Like Newport's oceanside Cliff Walk, Bar Harbor's Shore Path is a long public walkway that skirts the rocky coastal ledges and overlooks Frenchman's Bay and beyond to the procession of hump-backed islands called the Porcupines.

In a line with other rambling Shore Path cottages—as Maine summer houses are called after the early hotel guest cottages—the Reef Point cottage was built in 1883, one of twenty-two buildings designed in Bar Harbor by the Boston firm of Rotch & Tilden, which specialized in a combination of flat log and shingle construction with turrets, high gables and dormer windows as well as wide verandahs. By the time the house was completed, Beatrix's parents were already separated and the property signed over to her mother. Although the land is now divided among five residents, the configuration of the perimeter has remained surprisingly intact. To all appearances, it is possible to walk to the end of Hancock Street in the silence of a summer afternoon and stand in front of the granite gate pillars and finials of Reef Point under towering white spruce as though nothing had changed. A curved entrance drive leads to the picturesque Gardener's Cottage, one of the few buildings to survive the demolition of the gardens. A short stroll along the lichen-covered white cedar boundary fence on the Shore Path gives a sense of the dramatic views across the water which determined the axes of the fanned-out garden paths.

Max and Beatrix Farrand at Reef Point

Preserved among Beatrix Farrand's papers at the University of California, Berkeley, is a bound journal from her early twenties with the printed title *Book of Gardening*, in which she recorded from October 10, 1893, to May 31, 1895, her observations about horticulture and garden design both in America and abroad, mostly in Italy and Germany. In addition to noting her critical impressions of a visit to the grounds at Fairsted, Frederick Law Olmsted's office and residence in Brookline, Massachusetts, and of gardens at the 1893 World Columbian Exposition in Chicago, she expressed in early entries her appreciation of the details that made Reef Point and Maine a magical place and the center of her life.

"The scarlet trumpet honeysuckle over the porch has small bunches of scarlet berries all over it which make it as effective as in the blooming season." This description of what she later called "vertical flower beds" is of a piece with the Bulletin she wrote sixty years later on climbing plants. Tutored privately, Beatrix Farrand developed early on a keen sense of observation and taste as well as a distinct writing style that rendered her ideas and opinions as clearly as if she had drawn them in a detailed plan. Like many Maine summer residents, she returned to view the autumn color in a ritual not without its melancholy side. Among pressed leaves and sketches for the alignment of trees, she wrote, "I noticed the coloring of the leaves more beautiful than ever . . . this season before we left." Despite Maine's harsh climate, nature always conspires to make one's day of departure the most inviting.

Since the majority of Mrs. Farrand's voluminous writings are in the quasi-public form of reports to or correspondence with clients, these journal entries provide a rare opportunity to look over her shoulder in a private moment. Her descriptions of gardens prove to what degree observation was the foundation of her education. During the early 1890s, she was guided in this technique during her training in horticulture and landscape gardening at Harvard University's Arnold Arboretum under the tutelage of Charles Sprague Sargent, its first director. The source of Professor Sargent's oft-quoted advice to her—"make the plan fit the ground and not twist the ground to fit a plan"—is found here in the final Bulletin, an autobiographical account intended as her obituary. She continued to forge links with the Arboretum over the years, frequently seeking advice on the specific identification of plants, which were carefully packed and mailed from Bar Harbor to Jamaica Plain.

In traveling abroad, Beatrix was often in the company of her aunt Edith Wharton, her father's sister, who in 1904 published her own travel impressions in the quintessential *Italian Villas and Their Gardens*, many years after her niece's journal was written. During this period, the specifics of European gardens recorded by professionals and Grand Tour travelers became the new grammar of American estate gardens as designed by Beatrix Farrand and her contemporaries. Although the divorce of Beatrix's parents may have altered the path of her life in New York society, the dynamic relationship among the three women—the vivacious mother, the daughter and the aunt, only ten years Beatrix's senior—provided the catalyst for a secure, confident and independent life. Being different was in a sense also liberating. Her cousin and adviser, John Lambert Cadwalader, was also part of the family equation. A lawyer and founder of the New York Public Library, his picture was placed over a mantle at Reef Point, where Beatrix Farrand once showed it to a young friend, saying, "He is the person I have been closest to in my life." Cadwalader encouraged her early on to a career in landscape gardening which she pursued for over fifty years—completing nearly two hundred commissions—with unswerving determination and efficiency.

During the winters, until she married in 1913, Beatrix Farrand lived with her mother at 21 East 11th Street. Like the gateposts of Reef Point, the five-story brick town house with its high stoop makes real the comings and goings of that early professional life which began in a top floor office as early as 1895. (Eventually, her office was moved to 124 East 40th Street.) Often, while she worked upstairs, Henry James was their house guest below. "My liveliest interest attends her on her path," he once wrote in a letter to Beatrix's mother. In 1899, at a meeting called to organize the American Society of Landscape Architects, she was the only woman present among the ten founding members.

On April 7, 1917, Mary Cadwalader Jones signed over Reef Point to her daughter by deed of gift, and from this point on, Beatrix and Max Farrand began building a personal institution that married their scholarly and horticultural interests. In reviewing any one project in her range of accomplishments (which included university campuses such as Princeton and Yale and private gardens for the Rockefellers and J. P. Morgan—and for the White House during the Woodrow Wilson administration), the researcher is always struck by the single-mindedness of the correspondence and reports, implying an exclusivity, as if nothing else could have mattered in her life at the time. But the reality is that Reef Point was the permanent underlying warp of the tapestry on which the weft of her other gardens was woven. Because their winter residence shifted from New Haven, where Max Farrand was professor of history at Yale, to San Marino, California, where he was appointed the first director of the Henry E. Huntington Library and Art Gallery, Reef Point became the main home for their libraries and art works as well as their gardens.

Like creative innovators of any century who are said to be ahead of their time, the Farrands conceived of a long-range plan for Reef Point which promoted ecological objectives that today are de rigueur for any institution concerned with land use. Founded in 1939, the Reef Point Gardens Corporation established a study center "to broaden the outlook and increase the knowledge of a small group of hand-picked students who are in training to become landscape architects." Beyond the gardens and library of Reef Point, Mrs. Farrand noted that Mount Desert Island offered other laboratories for the study of New England flora and "the ecological adaptation of plants to the environment." These included Acadia National Park, along with its issues of design and management, and the private gardens of the area, over fifty of them designed by Mrs. Farrand herself.

In the history of garden design, the influence of Reef Point Gardens as a personal expression of horticultural taste and design may be compared to such other pivotal gardens as Gertrude Jekyll's Munstead Wood and William Robinson's Gravetye Manor, both of which Beatrix Farrand visited in England. It was modern in the sense that its design did not allude to any historical style but was instead an enhancement or an elaboration of the natural features of Maine, such as the native bunchberry (*Cornus canadensis*), for example, which grew in dappled sunlight at the entrance to a wood. But her gardens also possessed components necessary to a botanic garden: systematic classification of plants of a single species; an herbarium of almost 1,800 pressed plants, created for scientific study; and micro-environments specific to the coast of Maine, such as a bog filled with purplish pitcher-plants. With the gardens charted into sections and the plants labeled, the scientific scope of Reef Point—yielding a disciplined design with its own harmonies of color, texture and form—was akin to those early botanic gardens founded by professors and physicians at medieval universities.

To give the illusion of a larger terrain as in eighteenth-century English landscape gardens, Mrs. Farrand devised a circuit of curvilinear paths that intersected the straight axial paths radiating toward the views. Guests were conducted along a preordained route so that the gardens unfolded in a succession of experiences: the vine gardens on the house; the rose terraces with the single varieties that were her passion; the rhododendrons and laurels on the way to the vegetable enclosure with its espaliered fruit trees; the perennial beds across the turf from the rock gardens; and past the pink azaleas, holly hedges and heathers to the bog. Surrounding these areas were stands of red and white spruce, planted in tight clusters as barriers to the severe winds, while other trees were allowed to grow free standing to retain the spread of their "youthful outlines." And twin Alberta spruce, one of her signature choices, stood as sentinels at the head of the paths leading to the bay. From the shore, this skyline appeared like "the great army of the pointed firs, darkly cloaked and standing as if they waited to embark," which Maine novelist Sarah Orne Jewett described so memorably in *The Country of the Pointed Firs* (1896).

Within the gardens were certain Arts and Crafts style ornaments reflecting not so much indigenous crafts but the work of others like herself, in particular Eric Ellis Soderholtz, whose tastes were formed on European travels. Born in Sweden, Soderholtz was an architectural draftsman and photographer in Boston who had made a survey of ancient art and architecture during a Grand Tour of southern Europe. After settling near Bar Harbor in West Gouldsboro, he devised a method of fashioning classical oil jars and amphorae out of reinforced concrete that could withstand the harsh elements. Hand finished, sometimes on a wheel, with slight pigment and incised ornamentation, these dramatic containers still grace many gardens in the area. (Lunaform, a craft studio in Sullivan, Maine, carries on this technique and also reproduces Soderholtz's original designs.) Two of his oil jars were positioned on either side of the main pathway at Reef Point (page 41), and his birdbath in a bed of heather (page 29) was the central feature of the lower garden. In addition to rustic benches placed strategically throughout the gardens for the views, there was one formal bench positioned under the eaves of the entryway (page 17). With multiple spindles turned on a lathe, its elaborate structure blended with the architecture of the house and its vine-covered walls. In reproduction, it is known as the Reef Point bench.

Although their lives were very different, Mrs. Farrand created a seaside garden that can be seen in direct relation to the flower beds Celia Thaxter cultivated next to her porch on Appledore Island off the southern coast of Maine. (In Mrs. Farrand's files is a note she once scribbled to herself about Mrs. Thaxter's 1894 book *My Island Garden*.) Mrs. Farrand may have crisscrossed the country and traveled abroad to design gardens for clients on a grand scale, with walled enclosures and formal garden rooms linked by naturalized plantings to woodland and wilderness areas beyond. But at Reef Point, she did what she loved most by creating a Maine garden of apparent simplicity where families of plants laid out in drifts meshed with others in a studied asymmetry. In addition to designing and constantly rearranging the plantings, she planned every aspect of the daily life at Reef Point, preparing for the big day when the establishment would stand on its own. The truth is that the pinnacle reached at Reef Point during this period was its great moment.

The Annual Reports she presented to her Board of Directors are the behind-the-scenes companion narrative to these Bulletins. They included horticultural developments, the titles of books acquired for the library and lists of seeds received from botanic gardens around the world as well as of plants culled from wilderness areas such as Mount Katahdin in Maine. In them, she never failed to thank the Garlands, her secretary, Isabelle Stover, and her French personal maid and expert flower arranger, Clementine Walter, who greased the wheels of an enterprise that valued the perfection of the domestic arrangements as much as the gardens.

The influence of Beatrix Farrand's life is still fresh in Maine, where the younger generation in her time have become leaders in the community, one that is still divided in a friendly way between local residents and summer people. David Rockefeller, who was a child when Mrs. Farrand designed his mother's garden in Seal Harbor, recalls her as "the epitome of a New England grande dame in a long dark dress and hat—tall, erect, austere, sure of herself, opinionated and frightening to most people." And he remembers walking in her heather garden and how beautiful and completely unpretentious it was. The Rockefeller family still houses the four-wheeled buckboard carriage David's father, John D. Jr., drove through Acadia National Park with Mrs. Farrand at his side. Beginning in the late twenties, they made these excursions together to inspect the plantings and the design of the bridges along the fifty-seven miles of carriage roads that were his imaginative contribution to the park. Mrs. Farrand responded to these outings with closely typed "Road Notes," offering suggestions in her usual no-nonsense language, with the names of appropriate trees and plants—sweet fern, wild roses, sumac, goldenrod and bush blueberry—listed along with directions for how and where to plant them.

> On the south and west sides of the road opposite the view young spruce should be used, and later on, as pitch pine is available. The north slope of the hill could be gradually planted with these giving a splendid Chinese effect to this superb northern prospect. These pitch pine will never intrude on the view any more than they do on the Shore Drive where they add a great picturesqueness to the position. (November 4, 1930)

Throughout these Notes, she urged Rockefeller "to vary the road planting in height and quality and type of material, as these varieties are usually shown in natural growth." In a sense, like the eighteenth-century British landscape designer William Kent, Mrs. Farrand leaped the fence of Reef Point and saw the whole landscape as a native garden. When her directions were not followed, she expressed displeasure, particularly when trees were planted in straight lines. Nevertheless she wrote to Rockefeller in 1933, "Again I want to thank you for the way in which you are so consistently upholding my judgments and helping with the ease of carrying on the work to which I look forward as one of the great pleasures of the Island days." He, on the other hand, found pleasure in the results: "for the first time [I] could understand why you are so partial to wild cherries and pear trees. The blossoms certainly are lovely."

Every six months, Mrs. Farrand forwarded a detailed accounting of the number of drives and days in the field in addition to office consultations and stenography. With a few exceptions, the amount owed was always the same: "No charge." Rockefeller, of course, was deeply appreciative and enjoyed their teamwork "in the public interest" for the "beautification of Acadia National Park." "I do not know when I have spent an entire half day in so carefree and enjoyable a manner as last Sunday afternoon," he wrote in May 1929 early on in their long road correspondence. "To feel that I could talk as frankly as I did about park matters, with the perfect assurance that nothing that was said would go further, added much to my satisfaction and sense of freedom in the talk."

The collaboration was a close and dedicated one. Toward the end of the correspondence in 1941, and at the season's end, the two tried unsuccessfully to make a rendezvous for a final carriage ride up Day Mountain. Rockefeller responded with the courtly congeniality that characterized their rapport. "What ever happens to the world," he wrote, "Day Mountain will be standing next summer and I much hope we can drive up it then." Throughout their long association, however, neither abandoned a formality and reserve instinctive to them both. One August, Mrs. Farrand wrote: "It was only with what I thought great self-control that I passed you the other day on your way homeward from an evidently brisk walk. I wanted to stop and say how do you do to you and to tell you what a pleasure it has been to work over the lodges and their surroundings [in the park]." Horticulturists on the Island have observed what may still be traces of her handiwork in such selections as the American bittersweet (*Celastrus scandens*) around the bridges that serve as overpasses for the carriage roads, now being restored after years of neglect.

Involving though their work in Acadia was, their main project together, which entailed hundreds more letters written between 1926 and 1950, was the garden Mrs. Farrand designed for Mr. Rockefeller's wife, Abby Aldrich Rockefeller, in a spruce forest below the Eyrie, their hilltop house in Seal Harbor. One of Beatrix Farrand's major designs, the Eyrie garden is still in family hands. (Dumbarton Oaks for Mr. and Mrs. Robert Woods Bliss in Washington, D.C., is now owned by Harvard University.) Although Mrs. Farrand worked directly with Mrs. Rockefeller, the correspondence confirming verbal arrangements was always with her husband. In 1921, the couple had traveled to China for the opening of the Peking Union Medical College, which was supported by the Rockefeller Foundation. Culturally, the voyage was a galvanizing event in their life. Yellowing newspaper articles in a scrapbook at the Rockefeller Archive Center show the tiled pagoda-style roof of the college entrance which confirms the influence of this architecture on the structures of the garden. Inside a pink stucco wall coped with yellow tiles from the Forbidden City, the contours and harmonies of mossy woodland settings for sculptures from the Far East are juxtaposed with a Maine interpretation of an English flower garden in brilliant seaside hues. Passing from cool green paths through a Moon Gate into a two-level walled enclosure of concentric rectangular borders provides one of the richest garden experiences in America today. The Abby Aldrich Rockefeller Garden, as it is now called, continued under the stewardship of David and Peggy Rockefeller. They reinstated the central greensward in its present form, and Mrs. Rockefeller monitored the borders imaginatively by introducing new perennials and annuals.

Although no longer as complete as the Rockefellers', the garden Mrs. Farrand designed at The Haven in Northeast Harbor for Gerrish H. Milliken and his wife, Agnes, beginning in 1925, possesses a special aura today. Agnes Milliken was a close friend of Beatrix Farrand and consulted with her on matters concerning Reef Point; it was she who aided Mrs. Farrand in the acquisition of Gertrude Jekyll's papers in the late forties. In designing the Millikens' garden, Mrs. Farrand incorporated, more than in any other private commission, many of the themes that made Reef Point so distinctive. Looking out today over a field of purple heathers to glimpses of blue water between stands of pointed firs—and to white sails that appear and disappear behind the trees—one gets an exact sense of what she sought as perfection for Maine. Now owned by Gerrish H. Milliken, Jr., and his wife, Phoebe, the garden comes the closest to how Reef Point itself must have appeared in its prime. Along the entrance path to the rambling shingle house, there is another Reef Point touch: borders of heliotrope by the porch and white nicotiana along the path, the former with a heavenly fragrance by day, the latter radiant by night. Like her own terraces of native single roses at Reef Point, there is a long rose path leading to an open terrace and a vine-covered pergola with modified Tuscan columns, where Agnes Milliken would take tea in the afternoons. These pergolas also became a characteristic feature of Mrs. Farrand's Island gardens.

Following Max Farrand's death in 1945, his wife began taking measures to adapt Reef Point architecturally for its future. Robert Patterson was the architect, and in 1946 he completed the Gardener's Cottage for the Garlands employing many of Rotch & Tilden's decorative motifs from the main house. Mrs. Farrand describes other renovations and additions in the Bulletins themselves, including the new Garden Club House given by the Garden Club of Mount Desert, of which Mrs. Farrand was the founder in August 1923. By the summer of 1947, the establishment was at a peak of activity: books and papers were catalogued daily; herbarium specimens were collected and pressed; new species arrived to be recorded and planted; and, of course, visitors were coming on a regular basis. In the end, over fifty thousand people had visited Reef Point on its open days. On one occasion, young sailors from a warship in dock came for tea and cakes in the garden. Despite the depression and World War II, Reef Point survived in a mode that combined the most advanced thinking in scientific and educational techniques with a kind of gracious Edwardian summer life.

Donald E. Smith, a gardener at Reef Point during summers in the early fifties while he was a horticulture student at the University of Maine, recalls the routines as everyone did his or her tasks in the garden overseen by Mrs. Garland. Often Mrs. Farrand surveyed the scene from her balcony. "She always wore Harris tweeds even in the summer and walked around the gardens with a cane and a shawl over her shoulders," he said. "She was very erect, very pleasant though stern, but we got along fine." Clementine Walter was the first one out in the early morning to hear the bird calls, and even Mrs. Farrand herself kept track of the birds' nests, especially a mockingbird's in the Alberta spruce. After his early training, Smith went on to work at Dumbarton Oaks, where he eventually became superintendent. Now in retirement, he lives in his wife's family's house down the street from Reef Point.

The event that caused a slow but not so subtle transition in this way of life came suddenly on October 17, 1947, when a fire that began smoldering in a cranberry bog spread fiercely with the wind to devastate the town of Bar Harbor and many of its elegant summer cottages. Although Reef Point was not affected physically, and daily life appeared to go on as usual, the character of the town began to change. Visitors more and more came as tourists in search of amusement rather than with notebooks in hand to look and learn. At that time, Mrs. Farrand wrote in her report to the Board: "Those who see the garden's visitors from the windows occasionally wish that fashionable scarlet coats would not pause too long minutes in front of lavender and pale pink flowers—but mercifully fashions change."

The Garlands, too, were getting older and becoming less active. In her search for someone with experience who could take over Mrs. Garland's responsibilities in the garden, Mrs. Farrand sought the advice of, among others, Thomas H. Everett, the chief horticulturist of the New York Botanical Garden. Everett, an Englishman, was on a speaking engagement at Wisley when he met Kenneth Beckett and subsequently recommended him to Mrs. Farrand. Beckett came to Reef Point for six months during the season of 1954; and in the Annual Report of that period, Mrs. Farrand praised him for his excellent propagating work in the greenhouse. But he never felt at home in Bar Harbor and eventually returned to England. During her California stay the following winter, Mrs. Farrand, then eighty-two, took realistic stock of her position. Costs were mounting, no guarantees could be made on a perpetual tax exemption or on the status of Reef Point Gardens as a foundation until after her death (Bar Harbor had lost much of its tax base as a result of the fire), and finally, and even more urgent, she feared the deterioration of the gardens.

From Mrs. Farrand's perspective in the early spring of 1955, if Reef Point Gardens with its ephemeral nature could not be maintained to her standards, she would rather see it destroyed. As usual, she made the courageous decision and took action immediately by writing to Robert Patterson to set the wheels in motion. Some of her associates, including the lawyers, were incredulous, but Mrs. Farrand was as determined now to put an end to the Gardens as she had been to create it. Together, the house and the gardens were sold for $6,500 to Patterson, who maintained a desperate hope that the gardens could be saved. There was no way of knowing then that Reef Point Gardens was ahead of its time by only fifteen or twenty years. A renewed interest in landscape architecture and environmental issues—the greening of America—got a fresh start in the 1970s on the heels of the consciousness-raising Earth Day celebrations. And the first major review of Mrs. Farrand's work came in May 1980 at a symposium at Dumbarton Oaks.

Having made her decision, Mrs. Farrand began to disperse possessions to friends. The young David Rockefellers, who badly needed furniture for their new houses, went to see her. "We told her of our plight," recalled David Rockefeller, "and she gave us first crack. We took almost ninety percent of what she had." Now scattered among many homes, they have become treasured mementos of the family's long friendship. Several pieces of fine glassware and furniture also went to the Milliken family. (And just how fine they were was proven with time. One Milliken daughter decided to sell the Philadelphia Chippendale wing chair with elaborate hairy paw feet which she had stored in her barn for many years. When it came on the block at Sotheby's in January 1987, it went for $2.75 million, thereby setting a record for the most expensive piece of furniture ever sold at auction. It had been ordered from the maker Thomas Affleck by General John Cadwalader, Mrs. Farrand's ancestor, and the carving was attributed to James Reynolds.)

The heart of Reef Point, as Mrs. Farrand called it, was the 2,700-volume horticultural library, along with its collection of documents and garden prints, and the herbarium. When Mrs. Farrand acquired the archives of Gertrude Jekyll, with over three hundred garden plans, plant lists and photograph albums, she called her "one of England's best horticultural writers and artist gardeners of the last hundred years." The Reef Point collection also included a donation made by Mary Rutherfurd Kay, a Connecticut garden architect, of her own notes, books and valuable slides. Mrs. Farrand was painfully aware that even were the collections to remain in the house, the conditions were damp and the facilities not fireproof. During the forties and early fifties, after receiving an honorary degree from Smith College in 1936, she donated to the Smith library over three hundred horticulture and landscape architecture books and many volumes each of more than one hundred periodicals in the same fields. One rare book, in John Evelyn's 1693 English translation, was *The Compleat Gard'ner; or, Directions for cultivating and right ordering of fruit-gardens and kitchen-gardens* by Jean de La Quintinye, the gardener of Louis XIV's kitchen garden at Versailles. In addition, she gave the college almost eight hundred literary titles, among which Jane Austen figured prominently. From 1938 to 1942, the Cambridge School of Architecture and Landscape Architecture in Cambridge, Massachusetts, had been a graduate school of Smith College.

As the future home for her collections, Mrs. Farrand sought an institution offering courses in "landscape art" and discovered that there were relatively few. Finally, to begin what she called their "new life under other skies and with wider opportunities for use," she selected the Department of Landscape Architecture at the University of California, Berkeley. The College of Environmental Design Documents Collection is located in Wurster Hall, the headquarters of the Departments of Architecture and Landscape Architecture. Today, the life in this building is extremely active and exciting with a constant parade of student projects and exhibitions pinned to the lobby walls. Here, in an educational institution where young people address environmental issues, the heart of Reef Point beats on.

After she sold Reef Point, Charles K. Savage, a member of Mrs. Farrand's board, came forward with an imaginative and ambitious solution for the future not of the gardens per se but of the rare plant collections, which he considered the finest in Maine. Savage was the owner of the Asticou Inn in Northeast Harbor. He was a special person in an unusual position. Deprived of a college education by the early death of his father, who was innkeeper before him, he sought every opportunity to educate himself in art, music and literature. His aesthetic interests and ambitions were recognized by the intellectuals among the summer residents, who lent him books and invited him to cultural events. Finally, he developed a talent for landscape design by reading widely in the field and becoming knowledgeable in all its aspects.

In a paper simply titled "The Moving of Reef Point Plant Material to Asticou," Savage proposed to document and then transport the Reef Point collection of azaleas, rhododendrons, laurels and heathers, along with other plant materials, across the Island to a site around a reflecting pond across the road from the Asticou Inn. Noting that "many features of the natural scenery of Mount Desert have similarities to the Japanese, particularly in the parts of the island where bold ledges, rocks and pitch pines prevail," he was inspired to create a stroll garden in the spirit of the famous water garden at Katsura Imperial Villa in Kyoto, which had "the same low stone slab bridge, mown lawns to the water's edge, azaleas and pines." This proposal was made to John D. Rockefeller, Jr., who paid the greatest tribute to Beatrix Farrand, his old friend and adviser, by supporting this project with an initial $5,000 to purchase the plants and with additional funds during the next few years to create the Asticou Azalea Garden and enhance the terraces and gardens at Thuya Lodge. Mr. Savage was already involved in developing the Thuya property above the Asticou Inn. This had been the home, library and garden of the Boston landscape architect Joseph Henry Curtis, who had died in 1928.

Charles Savage and his sixteen-year-old daughter, Mary Ann, made many trips together to Reef Point with a book of paint samples and colored pencils to list the azaleas and record their colors with a color chip or pencil mark. In one letter to Mr. Rockefeller he reported, "A great deal of my thought has been given to the arrangement of the trees and shrubs in this garden—mass, line and color, as well as the progression of azalea bloom—with the hope that the effect from the road as people pass by may be, (I hope), an outstanding one." Lewis Garland chauffeured Mrs. Farrand over in the dark blue Dodge every two weeks or so to view the progress of the garden, and she would get out of the car, remove her shawl and stand to talk with Mr. Savage for awhile.

Even the Alberta spruce were brought to the new homes. At Thuya, they have retained their natural form, while at Asticou one has been saved by expert pruning in the Japanese style. Many of the perennials were also planted in the Thuya Garden, so that together the two places have become the successors to Reef Point in an extraordinary feat of plant preservation. In early spring, when the azaleas are in bloom, the paths in the Asticou Azalea Garden wind through clouds of pastel pinks muted by melancholy mists from the sea. But Asticou is equally beautiful in summer, with its cool sand garden inspired by Ryoan-ji, also in Kyoto, and its subtle range of greens, and in autumn with its brilliant leaf colors.

Mrs. Farrand's gardens also continued in a more direct way. When the main cottage at Reef Point was dismantled (her old friend and executor, Judge Edwin R. Smith, lives on in the Gardener's Cottage), Robert Patterson incorporated entire sections of its interior into a new cottage he designed for her adjoining the farmhouse at the Garland family farm on the main road near Salisbury Cove, where Lewis and Amy Magdalene Garland had retired. The team then stayed together, for Clementine Walter lived with Mrs. Farrand in her house. The charming gray white clapboard cottage with peaked roofs had three major rooms—two bedrooms with a sitting room between them—that faced the back, and the tripartite rear facade reflected this arrangement. Each of the three rooms had French doors that opened onto its own section of the garden terrace. Outside the bedrooms, perennials from Reef Point were planted in rectangular beds with annuals around the edges, and heather mixed with lavender thrived along a serpentine path leading from a millstone by the sitting room door. The gardening continued, with a subdued palette of pink, lavender and gray outside Mrs. Farrand's window, and brighter colors—red, yellow and orange—outside Clementine Walter's. The balustrade from the Reef Point vegetable garden with carved oak leaves formed an elegant barrier between the garden and the wild cherries and fields beyond.

Mrs. Farrand brought all of her favorites from Reef Point, including the *Hydrangea petiolaris*, which thrives today more than ever, covering the whole back of the barn. And her beloved single roses are crammed in wherever possible. Donald Smith remembers well his visits to her at Garland Farm, where she surrounded herself, just as she did at Reef Point, with myriad vases each holding a single rose. Even her local dressmaker, Mary H. Barron, continued to serve her at Garland Farm, although there was no more need for dresses like the one she made for Mrs. Farrand's sojourn to Boston in the 1930s to take tea with King George VI and Queen Elizabeth. "The Scotch tweeds she brought with her each summer for suits," recollected Mrs. Barron, "were so rough the briar burrs were still in them." Most of her suits were in a mixture of black, white and gray, although there was one exceptional soft purple tweed, and all of the blouses matched the jacket linings and were made with sleeves full enough so that when she pointed, the fabric would not fall back and reveal a bare arm. In later years, she was never without her distinctive black ribbon choker.

When Mrs. Farrand died on February 27, 1959, her service, by her own request, was attended only by Robert Patterson and the small loyal band at Garland Farm. Her ashes were scattered, like her husband's. But the garden at Garland Farm, her only truly private garden, has survived. The Goff family, who lived there between 1970 and 1993, were meticulous in overseeing it. Helena E. Goff, who was president first of the Bar Harbor Garden Club, and later of the Garden Club Federation of Maine, Inc., took on the mantle of responsibility to maintain Mrs. Farrand's last garden, with occasional visits from Mrs. Garland. When the house was sold after the death of his parents, Jerome I. Goff became guardian of Mrs. Farrand's last remaining papers in the house, including her treasured collection of seed packets from botanic gardens and plant societies around the world. The current resident of the cottage, Virginia Dudley Eveland, has engaged two local women landscape gardeners to maintain the gardens in pristine condition, including the fenced-in rock garden in front with its profusion of ginger and other Far Eastern–style plantings. Although the Garland Farm garden is small, a review of the plant labels indicates that all the important ones are there—a microcosm of the much larger world Mrs. Farrand inhabited.

The memory of Reef Point Gardens as it was, though, is guaranteed only by this written record. Publishing the Bulletins in this complete form is tantamount to re-creating in depth the multifaceted endeavor of Reef Point which was supported by a devoted staff whose standard of excellence gave her joy. Read together, they constitute a descriptive account that both restores the gardens in their visual form to the mind's eye and summarizes the knowledge and experience of a lifetime.

Beatrix Farrand lived by a Latin motto inscribed first in the hallway at Reef Point and later at her Garland Farm cottage: "Intellectum da mihi et vivam" (Give me understanding and I shall live). Her own intellect is at the center of these texts, and her goal was simply to impart knowledge that would increase the reader's appreciation of gardens and natural landscapes. "The added happiness to life given by an interest in outdoor beauty and art has a very distinct bearing on a community," she wrote in her 1939 prospectus for Reef Point. There is also in these essays an echo of a frequent expression found in her letters from Maine: "At last I have reached home again . . ." For within these pages, the gates to Reef Point Gardens are always open.

PAULA DEITZ

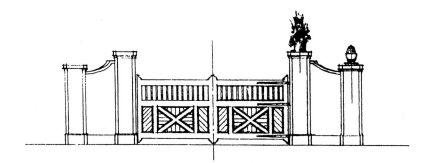

REEF POINT GARDENS BULLETIN

Copyright, 1946, by Reef Point Gardens

PUBLISHED BY THE MAX FARRAND MEMORIAL FUND

BAR HARBOR · MAINE

Vol. I   No. 1   *AUGUST*, 1946   Price 10 cents

WALK TO GARDEN

The Start and the Goal.

MORE Than Sixty Years Ago the parents of the present owner of Reef Point bought two acres on the Shore Path and built a cottage. They first intended to use the house for only two or three summer months but the family became so attached to the house and its surroundings that the seasons lengthened from two or three months to nearly half the year. At the same time the acreage was also enlarged as two acres were added to the south of the original holding, and later still two more acres were added to the north.

The years passed, and Mary Cadwalader Jones, the owner, gave house and land to her daughter and her daughter's husband as their home. Beatrix and Max Farrand grew to care for Reef Point increasingly and it became more and more truly their chosen home. A family tradition of gardening and a growing interest in all plant surroundings, caused the owners as they worked over their grounds to consider later development of the little acreage.

As Max and Beatrix Farrand thought of the various possibilities for the future of Reef Point they decided after several years of careful study and legal and horticultural consultation to plan a permanent future for the place they had greatly enjoyed. Reef Point Gardens was therefore incorporated under the general laws of the State of Maine in August, 1939, and a group of members, officers and directors elected, and arrangements made to provide an adequate endowment in the future. Although the corporation does not yet hold any property except a small bank account, it has been recognized by the Federal authorities as a philanthropic and educational institution and its purpose is many-sided.

The object at Reef Point is primarily to show what outdoor beauty can contribute to those who have the interest and perception that can be influenced by trees and flowers and open air composition. Such interest is never likely to diminish and a taste for gardening can add much to life. Intimate contact with growing things, observation of passing seasons and changes give interest and flavour to each day. Wise use of leisure is a problem for each individual to solve, but Reef Point Gardens hopes to be of use as a living example of at least one of the many solutions.

Another facet is the educational side. This is not being neglected, as the important trees are being labeled, records made of all plantations, and notes kept on individual plants. Files of notes and records will be open to students who wish to consult them. In addition to the records and files a small working library is being assembled for the future.

On the practical side a small vegetable garden contains an orchard of dwarf fruit trees, peaches, apples and cherries, as it is the aim to make the gardens useful by example as well as precept. The kitchen garden is large enough to grow the smaller crops, and fruit and vegetables for a family of six or seven have been provided for the summer months.

As an illustration of what is possible even in a small space, flowers are grown near the house in terrace beds of moderate size. In these small areas flowers bloom from late March until November and all the plant material used is of modest cost, or grown on the place. In another part of the grounds hardy perennials are grown in a special garden, and here again the plants have been chosen for their beauty throughout the season rather than for a spectacular effect for a brief number of weeks.

As the local flora is of incomparable beauty, indigenous plants are encouraged. Carpets of bunchberries and bearberries are cared for, and native shrubs, whether seaside or woodland loving, are planted where they seem to thrive. Ground carpeting plants of many sorts are grown, and various types of soils have been used to show plants which will actually flourish in gravel or those which prefer acid or shade, and others which can endure full sunshine.

The original owners made many mistakes in their early gardening days before they learned by many a bitter lesson what nature had been trying to teach them. They found that if the normally acid soil conditions were acknowledged as an asset rather than a detriment, numberless plants would grow with astonishing enthusiasm. Rhododendrons and azaleas from many parts of the world have found a home, and surprising success has been achieved with Chinese and Asian shrubs and creepers. If the owners had been able to visit a trial ground such as Reef Point is at present they would have been kept from many an error of horticultural judgment.

The local Garden Clubs are often asked to share divisions or seedlings as a part of the usefulness of the Garden, and close collaboration is made with local schools. Classes from the High School visit the grounds with their teachers, and visitors from the horticultural department of the University of Maine are frequent and always welcome.

Reef Point Gardens is open daily to all who are interested in horticulture and in seeing trees, shrubs and perennials growing in informal plantations. It is open each and every day throughout the long growing season, and during the year 1945 over two thousand garden lovers visited the place.

When the directors of the corporation assume control of the Gardens and their endowment in the future, they will replace the present dwelling house with another building in which there will be a large room where garden clubs may meet, small flower shows be held, and lectures given on subjects allied to horticulture. The new building will also contain the working library and a few study rooms for those who wish to use them. As a further part of the educational side it is hoped to establish a few scholarships for students who wish to make themselves familiar with the beautiful and characteristic flora of this part of the state. Bulletins will be published from time to time about the plants growing at Reef Point, such as early flowering bulbs, azaleas, rhododendrons, dwarf fruit trees, ground covers, and so on, and these will be distributed or sold to arboreta and botanic gardens in this country and abroad, and also will be available to garden club members and horticulturists in general.

A training in appreciation of natural beauty and interest in bird and plant life seems desirable as a contribution to every community and each state. It is hoped that Reef Point Gardens may serve this purpose, as it is for this object that it has been started. Its goal is to be useful to its community and state, and to all interested in outdoor beauty.

BEATRIX FARRAND

REEF POINT GARDENS
Bar Harbor, Maine

OFFICERS
BEATRIX FARRAND, *President*
ALBERT HALL CUNNINGHAM, *Treasurer*

MEMBERS

ALBERT HALL CUNNINGHAM	JOSEPH MAGEE MURRAY
SUSAN DELANO MCKELVEY	ROBERT WHITELEY PATTERSON
GERRISH HILL MILLIKEN	SERENUS BURLEIGH RODICK
LAWRENCE MORRIS	ISABELLE MARSHALL STOVER

ROBERT AMORY THORNDIKE

DIRECTORS

ALBERT HALL CUNNINGHAM	GERRISH HILL MILLIKEN
BEATRIX FARRAND	LAWRENCE MORRIS

SERENUS BURLEIGH RODICK

4

THE MERRYMOUNT PRESS, BOSTON, U. S. A.

REEF POINT GARDENS BULLETIN

Copyright, 1947, by Reef Point Gardens

PUBLISHED BY THE MAX FARRAND MEMORIAL FUND

BAR HARBOR · MAINE

Vol. I   No. 2   *NOVEMBER,* 1947   Price 10 cents

SEWALL BROWN, PHOTOGRAPHER

SHORE FRONT OF REEF POINT GARDENS

Past Present and Future

THE past is fairly easy to reconstruct as the rocks on the eastern shore of Mount Desert Island tell their story for us to read. The formation is ancient as the oldest beds were once the sandy floor of an ocean which covered the whole area many millions of years ago. Through these beds of sandy mud the volcanoes of that period blew out ash clouds which hardened into the whitish layers seen at Reef Point. Later—much later—molten rock was thrust up through cracks and these intrusions formed the dikes which are conspicuous on the shore; there are several, the outer one forming the reef from which the place takes its name. At varying depths underlying the thin soil other dikes of volcanic rock lie hidden; these run parallel to those visible on the shore. They traverse the acreage from north to south and cut through the ancient sand and ash beds. Finally the dikes were baked by the nearby molten granite which forms the range of mountains lying across the whole Island.

At one time there must have been a watercourse running eastward into the little northerly cove. This is indicated by a layer of stiff glacial clay underneath the present bog. In later geological time ice covered the Island, and glaciers from far away in the north deposited alien rocks and boulders and as they dragged their gravelly bases over the old formations they made parallel scratches and tiny "chatter marks" which may still be seen on one or two of the visible pink dikes.

Even in one little lifetime the aspect of the shore has changed. Some of the big volcanic walls have split and fallen, overturned by thrusts of ice in the fissures, and battering of the sea on softer strata. Part of the easterly point has collapsed and walls are needed to halt the hunger of the waves. Many more millions of years passed before the land took on its present expression and became clothed with vegetation, but the aspect of today is formed by the underlying rocks and the soil made by their disintegration and the deposit left by the ice sheet.

Building of soil is a long process often needing centuries for accretion, therefore the present thin coat must have been accumulating for many years before it became fertile enough to support the growth of trees and shrubs which in their turn fed and protected the ground in which they grew. The foothold for plants became more favourable as the soil deepened and gradually the present plants began to appear, some carried from regions in the Arctic.

In the early days of human settlement there must have been an Indian village near Reef Point, as a stone implement was found near the shore in a heap containing many clamshells. When the white settlers came they made winding paths through the evergreens which grew thickly in spite of shallow soil, as the moist sea air and cool nights were to their liking. The present owner found a grove of big red spruces straggling over the eastern half of the acreage; most of these have followed their predecessors, but even today a few survivors show the size of the old seaside forest. Many old trees have yielded to a younger generation, and white spruces have replaced the old reds on nearly the whole waterfront, but the reds are still holding their own on the west.

Sixty years ago fertile topsoil was almost entirely lacking. The roots of the big spruces spread over the ledges and under their branches a meagre covering of evergreen needles was varied by occasional streaks of red or white sand. In the course of a half century soil has been built up from almost nothing to a covering neither rich in composition nor generous in depth but at least sufficient to nourish many different ground-covers. Ferns, bunchberries and goldthread have replaced the thickets of rust-infected blackberries and spindly half-starved wild roses.

As the soil gradually improved under kindly treatment experiments were started in planting a few alien shrubs. At first failures were far more frequent than successes as the owners were both self-willed and unobservant and did not heed the plainly indicated opportunities before them. Slowly they learned that it was safer and wiser to cast aside their own fancies or preferences and to adapt their plans to what lay before them awaiting proper use. The plants which now predominate are those which prefer acid rather than alkaline soil. This series is one of the loveliest of the plant world. The range is from the ground hugging bunchberry or dwarf cornel, bearberry and goldthread to the tallest of the rhododendron family, with heathers and huckleberries among those of middle height.

Work is being done toward establishing the plantations on a plan which has been successful for a number of years and therefore may be carried forward with reasonable hope of success. No one can read the future, but if the experience learned in the past is heeded the years ahead should continue to add beauty to the plant groups. From time to time they will need renewal and replacement and perhaps plant enemies may make certain sorts difficult or impossible to grow, but there will be a definite armature of design on which the later changes may be modelled.

Various memories or impressions may be carried away by different visitors, but even if only a few remember a certain harmony in plant grouping Reef Point Gardens will have done part of its work. It has helped its owners in the past and in the years to come it is designed to help others who have gardens, whether large or small.

———

The devastating fire which has wiped out much property and beauty in its home town makes it the more incumbent on those connected with Reef Point to carry on the work with gratitude for its preservation and new courage for the future.

BEATRIX FARRAND

November 1947

8

George Grady Press, New York

REEF POINT GARDENS BULLETIN

Copyright, 1948, by Reef Point Gardens Corporation

PUBLISHED BY THE MAX FARRAND MEMORIAL FUND

BAR HARBOR · MAINE

Vol. I   No. 3   *SEPTEMBER,* 1948   Price 10 cents

SEWALL BROWN, PHOTOGRAPHER

ENTRANCE GATE

The Plan of the Grounds

ALTHOUGH the present six acre unit of Reef Point Gardens has been gradually assembled from three different lots, all seem to fit into the same
pattern. The land is shaped rather like a clumsily made mitten without a
thumb; the eastern side at the top of the mitten is bounded by the sea, cottage
lots adjoin the area to the north and south, and beyond the gates at the ends
of Hancock Street and Atlantic Avenue the last houses stand near the western
boundary.

The six acres slope upward from east to west, the contours roughly following
the shape of the mitten; ridges of rock lie near the surface everywhere except
where an old glacial brook course runs northeasterly into a cove. This small
ice-gouged pocket is deep and beneath it lies a bed of glacial clay covered by a
layer of poorly drained mucky soil where bog plants thrive. There are deposits
of old silver sea sand near the shore, hidden here and there by a thin coat of
blackish peat, a condition much to the liking of the heath family. As the land
rises toward the west the soil coat is thinner but is nevertheless deep enough to
allow large trees to grow, and throughout the acreage drainage is perfect,
sometimes rather too good, except in the little boggy pocket.

The central lot was bought first and a rocky ledge about midway between the
sea and western boundary chosen for the house site; its placing was as inevita-
ble as the plan for the grounds, since landscape design must be controlled by to-
pography. A drive from the foot of Hancock Street was placed on the extreme
southwest corner, because the middle lot could only be reached by a right of
way across the western end of the adjoining one. The house was built in 1883,
and at that time a stable seemed as necessary as a garage today; therefore a
spur road led to a small building in the northwest corner of the property where
the gardener's new house now stands. The drive had to be built on easy curves
as the old four-seated buckboard required as much elbow-room as the longest
modern motor car; this was fortunate because the old oval opposite the front
door is large enough for present needs. Soon after the house was built a friendly
but unpleasantly far-sighted visitor inquired where the boundary lay; when
shown a near-by tree marking the southern line he innocently asked what would
happen if a new house should be built almost within arm's length. After the
underlying significance of this chance remark had been assimilated there
could be no ease of mind until the southerly two acres were added.

Most of the near-by seaside properties had already been cleared of native
shrubs and ground cover in order to make smooth and level lawns. The owners
of Reef Point were interested in native plants and welcomed the protection
given by trees and shrubs, and finally, neither wished to haul the large amount
of loam in order to make a lawn nor give it the constant after care. So the natural growth was fostered and footpaths following the land contours seemed
to place themselves naturally, and little by little the various sections showed

the way for later development. A walk from the house to the shore was as much needed as a road approach; then a second path toward the sea started the present pattern radiating from the south end of the house. These footpaths were crossed by others meant primarily for care and weeding of the plantations. A small undersized tennis ground at a little distance from the house gave lively pleasure in the early days, but as energies veered from tennis to gardening the court became a garden of perennials and annuals.

During the first years leaves and pine needles were vigorously raked off each spring and autumn, but the owners at last realized they were fighting their own gardening plans by sweeping away what nature was patiently trying to make into good soil. Since the lesson was learned more than forty years ago leaves and small waste have been saved, whether lying on the ground under the pine and spruce trees and fern beds, or carefully gathered and later returned to the land. The gradual accumulation of topsoil has had a marked effect on the design as formerly starved regions now nourish healthy plants. Certain areas were classed as "difficult children," since they refused to grow anything except a meagre crop of spindly trees and dilapidated juniper bushes. The present vegetable garden was one of these problem children, but it was soon realized that shelter from wind was as urgently needed as topsoil, therefore the kichen garden was given the first protection. A carefully designed high wooden fence was completely successful and before long dwarf fruit trees throve among the vegetables. Outside the fence tall trees were encouraged to grow on the north to give additional windbreak, and higher temperatures inside the enclosure proved the usefulness of the protection.

In the early days visitors to Reef Point were puzzled by the lack of a trim lawn stretching unbroken to the sea. Occasional delicately veiled remarks indicated a question as to whether the dominant trees and shrubs implied a spirit of economy, while others asked more openly why the type of planting had been chosen. As the years passed the owners learned to understand the conditions more intelligently and instead of forcing an unwilling site to resign itself to something for which it had no liking they studied the area and found out by many trials and frequent errors that certain plants would gladly grow where conditions were what they had silently and persistently demanded. Careful observation showed that azaleas liked the moisture from the sea and old silver sand under their feet; they were further aided by the wind buffer of the surrounding fence. Slowly and largely by rule of the gardener's green thumb many plants which had been sulky are now happily established on formerly unpropitious sites.

Fortunately there is variety of aspect and soil; in some places full sun, in others deep evergreen shade or dappled shadow under deciduous trees, and here and there sandy and peaty soil with occasional pockets of blue clay lying under gravelly slopes.

When the idea for a permanent future for Reef Point began to develop in the

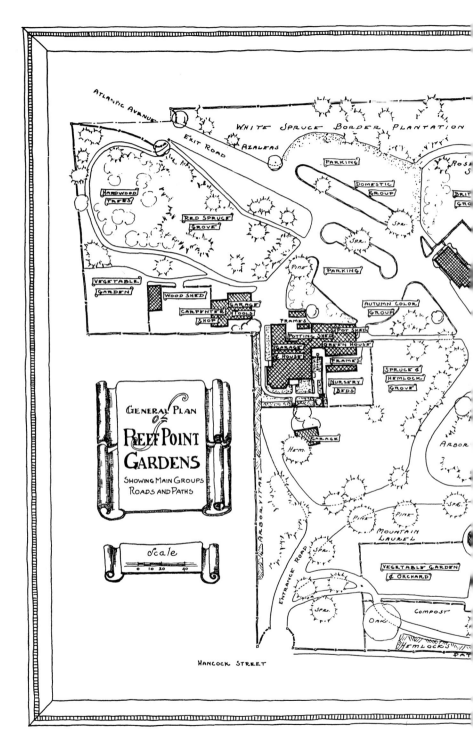

GENERAL PLAN
of
REEF POINT
GARDENS

SHOWING MAIN GROUPS
ROADS AND PATHS

Scale
0 10 20   40

ATLANTIC AVENUE
EXIT ROAD
WHITE SPRUCE BORDER PLANTATION
AZALEAS
PARKING
DOMESTIC GROUP
ROSE S
BRIT GRO
HARDWOOD TREES
RED SPRUCE GROVE
SPR.
SPR.
PINE
PARKING
AUTUMN COLOR GROUP
VEGETABLE GARDEN
WOOD SHED
GARAGE
CARPENTER SHOP
TOOLS
FRAMES
POT SHED
POTTING SHED
GREEN HOUSE
HOUSE
FRAMES
NURSERY BEDS
SPRUCE & HEMLOCK GROVE
GARAGE
HEM.
ARBOR
ARBORVITAE
PINE
PINE
MOUNTAIN LAUREL
SPR.
ENTRANCE ROAD
SPR.
VEGETABLE GARDEN & ORCHARD
SPR.
OAK
COMPOST
HEMLOCKS
PAT
HANCOCK STREET

12   PLAN

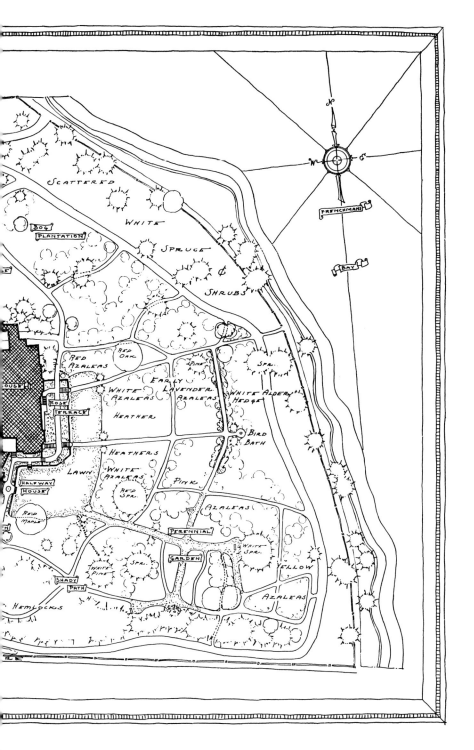

minds of Max and Beatrix Farrand they realized that if any considerable number of visitors were to be welcomed to the garden there must be easier access than provided by the original entrance drive and circle near the house: therefore when two acres to the north were added to the four at the south the design began to evolve. First the old driveway was altered in line and widened to ensure safe passing of vehicles; but it was kept as the main entrance since it allowed a convenient right-hand approach to both house and garden paths. Then on the northern acres a new road was constructed as an exit, and two spaces made for cars of visitors and guests. The new lot had long been neglected and the soil denied all nourishment; however, a small group of red spruce trees near the northern gate survived and the grove has been kept as an object lesson of the fortitude of native trees under adverse conditions.

When the house was built it was perched on top of a ledge sloping sharply eastward toward the sea; the front door on the southwest was reached on a level but the whole east side of the house looked perilously suspended in air as it was supported by piers connected by flimsy latticework. Shrubs and sundry other attempts to disguise the awkward change in level between the east and west sides of the building were not convincing; so finally the decision was made to build several small terraces following the varying grades as they increased in steepness on the sea side. Few notice today that the ground falls quite abruptly from the near-by street to the house site, and fewer still realize that the tops of the house chimneys are approximately level with the principal village street.

A professional workroom separate and yet connected to the dwelling by a passageway was clearly needed as the house was often littered with plans, catalogues and seed lists, accordingly, when material was available for its construction an office was built a short distance from the main building. A ground floor room was arranged for a secretary and the upper story made into a study, quiet, remote, yet conveniently near. On the north side of the house another passageway leads to a second garden house and gives access to the northern spaces, thus linking the main building to the two garden houses, the office and the parking ground. Physical conditions dominate the lines of the plan; the arc of buildings from north to south follows the curve of the sea front at the finger tips of the mitten. The shore path, open to the public, the near-by streets, and the neighboring houses are also controlling elements in the design.

The development of the western part of the acreage has come naturally because it was cut by entrances and paths; in one sense it is the least horticulturally important since considerable space had to be allotted to necessary working units, such as vegetable garden, roads and parking spaces, the gardener's house and adacent toolhouses and greenhouse, fertilizer sheds, cold frames, and a small cutting garden.

The most interesting plant groups lie on footpaths between the house and the shore. All are surrounded by a truck service road which follows the south, east and north boundaries. This road gives necessary and easy access to the various plantations and peat, compost, plants, gravel or stone are taken close to where they are needed. When this road was first discussed all agreed in thinking it was probably an extravagance and likely to be of little use, but to everyone's surprise it has developed into an essential artery and hardly a day passes without proving its usefulness.

The terrace shelves near the main building carry the most intimate and detailed planting. The earliest bulbs and latest flowers are here and from mid-March until late November there is colour, whether timidly appearing in earliest spring or gallantly withstanding the autumn frosts. An easterly terrace is planted with single roses where they enjoy morning sun and are shielded from hot southwest winds and afternoon heat. A small lawn finishes the setting of the main building below the little layers of terraces, and beyond the grassy space lie the larger groups—heathers in bright sunshine and sandy soil; ferns in a damper hollow, and groups of azaleas near the sea with other native and alien plants.

The flower garden lies behind a screen of trees, partly hidden and wholly protected. The borders are planted with perennials chosen not merely for attractiveness of flower but for character and beauty of growth and foliage. The plants are expected to be at least presentable when out of bloom and annuals are added here and there only to replace early sorts while later ones develop. Two or three paths lead to the garden, one in the deep shade of pine and spruce trees where acid soil loving plants are happy in the soft moist leaf mould under the evergreens; Christmas ferns, dog-tooth violets, goldthread, trilliums and gingers seed themselves and spread happily. A second path passes through a carpet of bunchberry, and a third in full sun crosses the heathers. The soil is gravelly to the north of the house; therefore several experiments have failed, but a group of the low-pasture juniper combined with the seaside species gives promise of good behaviour.

Years of close observation have shown that certain shrubs are contented in special positions—for example, groups of rhododendrons were set out where they are shaded from the low winter sun, and in another place dwarf deciduous and evergreen azaleas thrive in a situation akin to their native birch groves on Tibetan highlands.

Reef Point has been a part of its village for over sixty years and this close fellowship is valued; it wants to help local and visiting horticulturists who take an interest in their gardens and to welcome all who care for plants, birds and out-of-door beauty. In this way it hopes to take its place in the community and state. Those who are working at Reef Point will do their utmost to help Bar Harbor welcome visitors and friends as a mark of gratitude for preservation from destruction by the fires of last October.

BEATRIX FARRAND

September 1948

THE REEF POINT GARDENS CORPORATION
Bar Harbor, Maine

OFFICERS

BEATRIX FARRAND, *President*

ALBERT HALL CUNNINGHAM, *Treasurer*

ISABELLE MARSHALL STOVER, *Clerk*

Consultant

ROBERT WHITNEY PATTERSON

Members

ALBERT HALL CUNNINGHAM	LAWRENCE MORRIS
ARTHUR LOWELL DEERING	JOSEPH MAGEE MURRAY
BEATRIX FARRAND	ROBERT WHITELEY PATTERSON
DALE JOSEPH FOLEY	CHARLES KENNETH SAVAGE
SUSAN DELANO MCKELVEY	EDWIN RAY SMITH
AGNES MILLIKEN	ISABELLE MARSHALL STOVER

George Grady Press, New York

REEF POINT GARDENS BULLETIN

PUBLISHED BY THE MAX FARRAND MEMORIAL FUND

BAR HARBOR · MAINE

Vol. I   No. 4   *AUGUST*, 1949   Price 10 cents

SEWALL BROWN, PHOTOGRAPHER

FRONT DOOR REEF POINT GARDENS

The Buildings

THERE are fashions in architecture as well as in feminine raiment so when the kernel of Reef Point was built more than sixty-five years ago it corresponded to the mode of the day as expressed in the designs of Arthur Rotch, a Boston architect of repute. It was originally intended to be used for only a few months in summer in intervals of travel in Europe and long winters in New York. Sixty-six years ago when the house was started the picturesque was sought as eagerly as in the later years of the eighteenth century, consequently the cottage had a tower, several balconies, and many small dormer and "eye-winker" windows. The main lines were simple and good, and as it was always meant to be a part of a semi-woodland landscape it was quiet in colour and soon blended into the tree and shrub covered acres. It has always had the merit of subduing itself to the landscape rather than proclaiming its architectural importance, so that creepers and shrubs and little terraces have all become a part of the house picture. Houses invariably betray the likings of their owners and the uses to which they are put, and Reef Point has always shown it was a gardener's house as creepers and trained shrubs and flowers have surrounded it for many years.

In the later years of the nineteenth century houses were either shingled or clapboarded, so Reef Point was shingled from top to toe and stained either a bark brown or allowed to weather to a silvery grey, covered by a roof which lay in lighter grey folds over the windowed and balconied walls. The house was adequate for its original purpose, but as time passed the owners spent longer seasons at the place they grew to care for increasingly, therefore rooms had to be added, roofs raised and towers peeled off and balconies turned into full sized porches. Many of the rooms were deeply shaded by verandahs and not a ray of south sun reached the principal bedrooms and sitting room after early morning. This condition was quite tolerable during the hotter months, but when the family season lengthened from the original midsummer stay to an eight months sojourn it was evident that more sun was desirable.

Alterations have been made inside the house so that it will be ready for its future when the future becomes the present. Close to the entrance and opening to the east terrace a large sitting room is big enough for meetings of eighty or a hundred. Its walls are hung with a collection of French prints, mainly of formal gardens of Le Nôtre's design, but some of the smaller establishments are included. Many of the great gardens have now vanished, so Le Nôtre's portrait over the chimney-piece presides over many chateaux with which he was familiar but are now no longer in existence. The room is furnished simply but not "institutionally." The entire establishment—house and garden—is meant to show the kind of place an individual could live in, rather than a museum-like collection of linoleum paved rooms and bewildering grouping of botanical specimens in the garden. Nevertheless, the educational side of the enterprise has not been neglected. The hall running through the building from south to north follows the lead of the large room, with prints of Italian, Dutch, Spanish and other European gardens or palaces. The gay colours of the "Vues d'optique" brighten the entrance walls and while of little artistic merit they are interesting as records of garden and human fashions.

The library was the writing and work room of Max Farrand and since it is merely enlarged but retains the character he gave it with bookshelves, Hebridean rugs and furniture, it rightly bears his name. The library pictures are portraits of great botanists and writers like Linnaeus, and John Evelyn and Charles Sprague Sargent, or designers of distinction such as Gertrude Jekyll, Frederic Law Olmsted, and William Robinson. This library on the ground floor is destined to contain reference books, periodicals and current horticultural treatises. On one side of a north alcove there are cases for the Reef Point Gardens herbarium which will gradually be filled with specimens collected on the grounds.

The remaining ground floor rooms contain the working quarters: a small dressing room for women and another for men, a flower room, a kitchen and serving room. The basement and cellar are of course utility regions as the electric cables and panel boards, two furnaces and hot water heater take up practically all the space which had to be painfully excavated under the old house.

The second story is mainly devoted to a room containing the older books of the collection, such as bound volumes of old garden prints; books on garden design and history; and studies and illustrations of individual houses and their surroundings. This room will be used by special students of garden history, design or literature. There are also at present a few bedrooms on the second floor which will later be lined with book shelves for periodicals or special collections, such as the one containing the entire life work of Gertrude Jekyll. These study rooms will be reserved for students who wish to work on a specific problem related to the plant and library material at Reef Point.

Next in importance in any house arrangement is a provision for storage of unforeseen accumulations, so an attic over the main house has possibility of housing many boxes of papers and pamphlets, and spare furniture needed only for the larger assemblies.

Mr. Robert Patterson, the Reef Point consultant, solved the problem of keeping the outer face of the house virtually unchanged while cellar blasting was being done, steel beams placed under hanging partitions and chimneys rebuilt or perched on supports. All the tiresome technical structural design-ing was done by him so the owner had the fun of working over the details of a preparation and physical arrangement. The contractors were watchful and

SOUTHEAST VIEW 1883

SOUTHEAST VIEW 1948

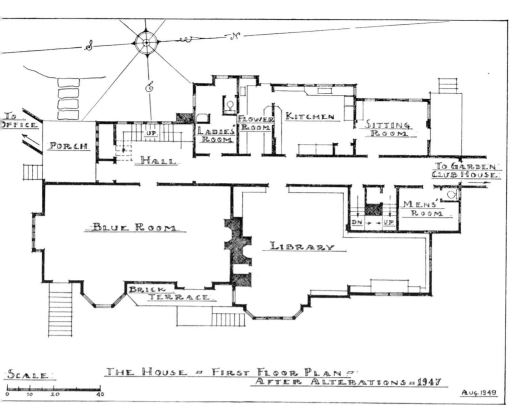

SCALE

0 10 20   40

THE HOUSE ~ FIRST FLOOR PLAN ~
AFTER ALTERATIONS ~ 1947

AUG. 1949

FLOOR PLAN 1948

GARDENER'S COTTAGE 1947

careful and in consequence not a creeper or plant was injured during the months of destruction and rebuilding.

The main house is connected by covered passageways to three smaller buildings. The southern one leads through a Half Way House with a quiet view over the garden to a two-storied office where the current records will in all likelihood be housed and where a secretary is ringed with files. Above stairs a good work room is perched above the kitchen garden, with an outlook eastward to the main house, its small flowering terraces, a corner of the lawn, and a triangle of Frenchman's Bay. Westward the dwarf fruit trees and vegetables and screen plantations bound the prospect.

On the other side of the main house the Northwest Passage continues the line of the house hall to the Garden Club House, given by the Garden Club of Mount Desert to the owners of Reef Point. This summer house is spacious enough for small meetings in warm weather, and as the view northeast over the upper bay is quite different from those to the south its prospect gives variety. A thirty foot terrace lies below the Garden Club House where visitors often come and spend a hot afternoon with books and enjoy the quiet harbour view.

The heart of the enterprise is of course in the main house, but no machine can run unless it be properly tended and wisely supervised. The housing of the head of the gardens is as essential a part of the future of the place as the main building. A new construction was designed by Mr. Robert Patterson and placed on the old stable and garage site at the northwest corner of the original two acres of Reef Point. Like the main house this dwelling is intended for all year living and has kitchen, dining, sitting room and a garage on the first floor and bedrooms above. As every housekeeper knows, the cellar, kitchen and closets are vitally important parts of any establishment; consequently these were arranged after many consultations with practical and accomplished house mistresses. This dwelling is part of a little group radiating from its centre and just as necessary in its practical way as the main house and its flock of satellites.

The potting shed, propagating lean-to and greenhouse are tied to the gardener's house by a Siamese twin attachment although there is no communicating door between these two units. The greenhouse is intended primarily for raising annuals for the summer brightening of the house terrace, but perennials are also started for garden replacements. A potting shed on the west connects the propagating bench to the greenhouse. These propagating facilities have proved of invaluable use. Seedlings of many cantankerous plants have been started and when they are out of the tiny fledgling stage they are moved to a set of north facing frames, corresponding to another set of south facing frames outside the greenhouse. Behind the greenhouse and alongside the propagating bench there is a utility house for pots, fertilizers, small sprayers and the larger tools.

22

Experience and many failures have taught the useful lesson that ample room is needed in toolhouse, workshop and rubbish yard if a garden is to be kept tidy. If space is not conveniently at hand it is always possible to say to oneself that there is no place to put a tool away and it is laid aside, sometimes under a bush or behind a rock and gradually it rusts away.

Further to the northwest another work building houses a garden truck and a compartment for the small tools, such as shovels, rakes, stakes, and weeding baskets. Behind these two divisions a well lighted workshop runs across the west end of the construction, where a workbench is placed with a tiny and most efficient stove and its accompanying chimney. This little stove does welcome service on many a chilly and cold day. Its inexpensive feed is scraps of lumber and bits of tree wood which heat many a dinner in winter weather.

The long catalogue of constructions is nearly finished, only two more remain to be noticed; one a lumber shed in the compost yard west of the work building where the many odds and ends of valid wood are put under cover. During the rebuilding of the main house there were leftover pieces of planks and lumber too sound to throw away and yet not of any immediate use. These are piled in the lumber shed and from these scraps emerge packing boxes, screens for windows, the heavy blocks and timbers for transplanting, and the countless odds and ends needed in a busy establishment. A small building near the gardener's house was the catch-all for surplus doors and windows during the remodelling of the house, and this little construction may later be used for a garage if a further car is needed.

The building alterations and the new work has been carefully considered with a view to future usefulness as part of an establishment founded to encourage the art of gardening and to help horticulturists and plant lovers of the Acadian region. The work has been done with care and all engaged have given it their best thought and supervision. Now it is in good condition as thorough repairs have been made in the old house, where new roofing and plastering, flooring and plumbing has been done and a complete heating system installed.

No one is wise enough to see far into the future but advice has been not only sought but accepted and acted upon. The work of remodelling and rebuilding should give the Directors of Reef Point Gardens a valid and working unit for the years that lie ahead when the present owner no longer directs the daily activities. The building part of the enterprise is launched in the same belief that the rest of the place has been conceived—that there is a place in the world where those who are moved by outdoor art may study or enjoy books, gardens, birds, and the beauty of sky, sea, colour and the changing seasons—ever different and yet eternal.

BEATRIX FARRAND

August, 1949

THE REEF POINT GARDENS CORPORATION
Bar Harbor, Maine

OFFICERS

BEATRIX FARRAND, *President*

ALBERT HALL CUNNINGHAM, *Treasurer*

ISABELLE MARSHALL STOVER, *Clerk*

Consultant

ROBERT WHITELEY PATTERSON

Recorder

MARION IDA SPAULDING

Directors

ALBERT HALL CUNNINGHAM

BEATRIX FARRAND

LAWRENCE MORRIS

CHARLES KENNETH SAVAGE

EDWIN RAY SMITH

Members

ALBERT HALL CUNNINGHAM

ARTHUR LOWELL DEERING

BEATRIX FARRAND

DALE JOSEPH FOLEY

SUSAN DELANO McKELVEY

AGNES MILLIKEN

LAWRENCE MORRIS

JOSEPH MAGEE MURRAY

ROBERT WHITELEY PATTERSON

CHARLES KENNETH SAVAGE

EDWIN RAY SMITH

ISABELLE MARSHALL STOVER

24

GEORGE GRADY PRESS, NEW YOR

REEF POINT GARDENS BULLETIN

Copyright, 1950, By Reef Point Gardens Corporation

PUBLISHED BY THE MAX FARRAND MEMORIAL FUND

BAR HARBOR · MAINE

Vol. I No. 5	*JULY*, 1950	Price 10 cents

SEWALL BROWN, PHOTOGRAPHER

LIBRARY CHIMNEYPIECE

The Max Farrand Library

T HE reference library on the ground floor at Reef Point bears the name of a distinguished scholar and historian, since he used it for much of his work. The furnishing and arrangements of the room are as they were made for him, as the Hebridean rugs were especially designed and they are, by his wish, an integral part of the composition. The original room has had its boundaries enlarged in order to give easy access to the various elements now housed within its walls, and herbarium cases, plant records and files take up most of the space in the new north alcove. The herbarium is an essential part of the room, as the plants pressed and mounted in their files will give students definite information regarding the material grown in the six acre garden. Eventually there may be more than fifteen hundred sheets in the cases, as each specimen must be shown in flower and fruit. Near the plant records it is planned to have a catalogued file of items of interest to gardeners and designers. Some of the scraps may be printed extracts from gardening papers relating to cultivation or soil preparation, while others will be illustrations of garden features, whether balustrades, steps, fountains, summer houses or plants. This material will be cross-filed so that students may find fences, benches and related subjects which may also be listed under other elements shown in the same illustration. It will take time to complete the herbarium, and still more time to arrange in orderly fashion many hundreds of pictures and clippings now awaiting orders to take their places in the work room. The room itself is not large, but it has a pleasant view over the sea and is well lighted. The walls are either panelled or shelved from floor to ceiling and in order not to give an institutional aspect to the study, comfortable chairs are part of the furnishing. Portraits of botanists or gardeners hang in friendly assemblage where wall space permits: Gertrude Jekyll and William Robinson follow their forerunner John Evelyn; while near by Linnaeus holds in his hand his namesake flower, the Linnaea of cool northern woods.

The books on the shelves may seem an oddly assorted group, as they range from the Encyclopaedia Britannica, the Dictionary of National Biography and Smith's Classical Dictionary to the large Oxford English Dictionary. If a questioning thought occurs as to why these great books of final reference find a place in this room, the answer comes as quickly as the thought. Many a problem is solved each season, either as to the correct use of a word, or the dates of a botanist's life and his published work, or the name of a nymph in some old garden print and the forgotten river or woodland spring her statue commemorates. These solid reference books occupy most of one wall and near by is a group of architectural books of comparatively recent date. There are volumes relating to iron and brick work, and also to mediaeval and later stone and bronze ornament, country bridges, house furnishings—as household designs are often of use for garden furniture. Some books on Asiatic and European architecture are on the shelves, and palaces and garden designs from Mexico, Spain, South Africa, France and England sit quietly side by side with the simpler farms, inns, cottages, country churches and their churchyards. There are a few standard histories of architecture and records of past times in England and France, and occasional regional studies. In America old houses are reviewed and illustrated from Canada to Southern California.

One wall is reserved for periodicals and complete files are either already in place or being completed. The full sets of Rhodora, the English Alpine Garden Society, Arnold Arboretum Bulletins, Morton Arboretum Bulletins, and several others are shelved and the major part of the English Garden Magazine and the Journal of the Royal Horticultural Society. There is also a big table reserved for current horticultural magazines, some of which are merely of fleeting interest, and are therefore cut up for the files, and still others are consigned to a vast waste basket when their counsels seem to warrant this drastic treatment. One side of the north alcove is reserved for current horticultural books. There are treatises on individual types of plants, such as roses, chrysanthemums, primulas and bulbs: others deal with plant pests and the remedies therefor. There are a few nature study books and a group of bird identification volumes and a book or two on minerals and insects. A few simple star guides and studies of soils and their treatment have been added. Tree, shrub and climbing plant treatises are also a part of the collection of popular and more recondite types. One or two local floras find their places on these shelves and finally a large group of guide books. Some of these may seem to the casual visitor to have little reason for inclusion in this particular reference library, but a second thought will show the value of these records, both contemporary and of many past years. No explanation is needed for the inclusion of guide books of present years, as they describe the various neighbourhoods from the social and historical point of view, necessary as part of any local study. The older Baedekers, Murrays and Hares of European lands may need excuse made for them, but these will quickly be accepted when pages of the old Murrays of Spain are turned describing many a garden no longer in existence.

The use of this library is open to those who genuinely wish to consult the material, but the casual tourist will not be admitted as he would disturb students who may be working in the room. Readers' cards will be issued this summer to those who wish to make application to use the library. Each reader should be introduced by a person or an institution favourably known to those in charge of Reef Point. These readers' cards will be for one season and are renewable, but students who apply are asked to be indulgent, as some of the filing and cataloguing cannot be completed for a time. The library, like the garden, is intended to help all those who need horticultural aid and to contribute its mite to the art of living as expressed in gardening.

BEATRIX FARRAND

July 1950

THE REEF POINT GARDENS CORPORATION
Bar Harbor, Maine

OFFICERS

BEATRIX FARRAND, *President*
ALBERT HALL CUNNINGHAM, *Treasurer*
ISABELLE MARSHALL STOVER, *Clerk*

Consultant

ROBERT WHITELEY PATTERSON

Recorder

MARION IDA SPAULDING

Directors

ALBERT HALL CUNNINGHAM
BEATRIX FARRAND
AGNES MILLIKEN
LAWRENCE MORRIS
CHARLES KENNETH SAVAGE
EDWIN RAY SMITH

Members

ALBERT HALL CUNNINGHAM
ARTHUR LOWELL DEERING
BEATRIX FARRAND
DALE JOSEPH FOLEY
FAY HYLAND
SUSAN DELANO MCKELVEY

LAWRENCE MORRIS
JOSEPH MAGEE MURRAY
ROBERT WHITELEY PATTERSON
CHARLES KENNETH SAVAGE
EDWIN RAY SMITH
ISABELLE MARSHALL STOVER

AGNES MILLIKEN

REEF POINT GARDENS BULLETIN

Copyright, 1950, By Reef Point Gardens Corporation

PUBLISHED BY THE MAX FARRAND MEMORIAL FUND

BAR HARBOR · MAINE

Vol. I   No. 6   *AUGUST*, 1950   Price 10 cents

Rev. Marion Bradshaw, Photographer

THE GARDEN IN JULY

A Visit to Reef Point Gardens

REEF POINT GARDENS are open every day from eight o'clock in the morning until toward dusk to everyone interested in trees and flowers. Visitors in motor cars are asked to use the Hancock Street gate and the parking spaces beyond the house. Pedestrians will find both the Hancock Street and Atlantic Avenue gates open.

It is suggested that visitors should start their walk around the gardens at the Hancock Street gate where they will doubtless notice the woodland character of the driveway, shaded by large red spruce trees underplanted with native ferns and violets. A footpath diverging to the right leads to a wooden gate in the fence surrounding the vegetable garden and orchard of dwarf fruit trees. This gate is sometimes closed, but visitors are asked to open it and follow the path along the south side of the enclosure where they will see on the left rows of garden vegetables, bordered by small free-standing apple trees, with peach and cherry trees on the north and east fences. The building in the northeast corner of the fence is the office where necessary typewriters click and order files are kept.

The gate in the southeast corner leads to the woodland garden, and if on leaving the kitchen garden a sharp turn to the left is made it will take the visitor to the little garden of plants growing in gravel and stones. A rock garden would be too ambitious a title but there are many plants of interest as well as those commonly known. Among the rarer ones are alpine and arctic willows (Salix tristis and herbacea) and the familiar ones will be recognized in carpets of thyme and juniper and patches of dwarf iris, "hens and chickens" (sempervivums) and dwarf lavender.

In the corner between a big native thuja and the circular office there is a group of the less well known evergreen rhododendrons such as the Chinese decorum and the Caucasian Smirnowii against a hemlock background, and smaller plants like the deciduous white and rosy-pink rhododendrons—mucronatum—are huddled against a dwarf English yew and bordered by violets of different sorts mixed with galax and wintergreens.

The narrow terrace on the sea side of the south garden house is intended to have something in bloom in each of the growing months. In early spring, often in late March, the first snowdrops are in bloom under the south wall of the main house. As the season advances tulips and later flowering bulbs take their positions and early in summer the bulbs and perennials are interplanted with annuals. An effort is made to have something in bloom on these small terraces from early till late, and as they are only about three feet wide they should show owners of small gardens what can be done in restricted space. From the middle of the south garden house (The Half-Way House) the grass path shows the way to the perennial garden, crossing the lawn and passing a group of apricot coloured June flowering azaleas and several fine Japanese and dwarf English yews, together with ground carpeting plants. The garden is intended to show perennials of consistently good foliage, therefore the choice is limited by this rigorous condition. There are groups of perennial geraniums, iris of sundry sorts, phlox, astilbes and their cousins the ulmarias, and in the yellow borders sunflowers, globe flowers, yellow aconites and double celandines carry the late summer colour.

Azaleas, which are really deciduous rhododendrons, are at their best in May and June; the eastern plantations consist mainly of yellow, orange and scarlet sorts, while the pinks are planted to the north. A walk leaving the northern end of the garden lies between the pink azaleas through hedges of winterberry (Ilex verticillata), lovely in late autumn when sprinkled thickly with scarlet berries. If this walk is followed a bog plantation of moisture loving plants will be seen on the left near the north Garden Club House: there are sweet gale (Myrica gale) Royal Fern (Osmunda regalis) Labrador Tea (Ledum groenlandicum) and a good many more small plants like bog cranberry and perennial forget-me-not. If the visitor will turn to the left toward the Garden Club House he will find seats on a terrace with pleasant views over the harbor and north bay. After a rest the British group may be noticed north of the house. These plants are such as the early settlers brought from home and among others an English oak, goldenchain, white rose of York, English privet and sweetbriar will be found undercarpeted by thyme and columbines. Junipers cover the lower hillside in order to show what may be grown on dry gravelly ground, and a border of rose species separates the junipers from the garden service road. The ground covers merit attention as there are nearly a hundred different sorts, evergreen and deciduous, but none are more continuously lovely than the native bunchberry (Cornus canadensis) which thrives at Reef Point, together with its companion the bearberry, both near the Garden Club House.

If the road toward the Atlantic Avenue gate is followed hedges of sweet scented old-fashioned lilacs will be noticed, screening the north and south parking spaces. Near the Atlantic Avenue gate and its planting of apricot azaleas, a woodland path diverges to the left, skirting the outer edge of the hardwood grove where there are May-flowering groups of daffodils and English bluebells and other shade loving plants such as hepaticas, foxgloves, mayapple, twinleaf and some of the woodland ferns. A small sunken path divides the hard and soft wood groves and this path turns into a trail through the red spruces and their completely different ground cover, and so to the south parking space. This parking space opens directly to the Garden Club and main houses, where climbing plants are grown on the walls—honeysuckles, hydrangeas, akebias, clematis and vines. A group of evergreen rhododendrons at the service entrance is made up of the white varieties of Catawbiense, and in June their flowers are at their best.

If the visitor is still unwearied, he may walk through the entrance porch at the southwest corner of the house and may notice whatever plants may be seasonally placed there, hostas and ivies in the early season, and later annuals, lilies, pelargoniums and perhaps a few coolhouse plants such as fuchsias. These again are varied in the late season by chrysanthemums and ivies "never sere," which last until the hard winter frosts.

The inner round of the gardens starts at the south porch and crosses the small terrace sheltered by the house. Here the "earlies" bloom and are fol-

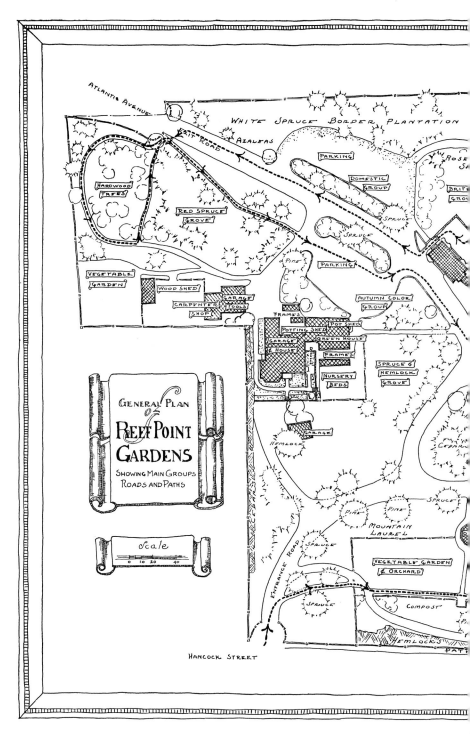

General Plan
of
Reef Point
Gardens

Showing Main Groups
Roads and Paths

Scale

0 10 20   40

Atlantic Avenue

White Spruce Border Plantation

Azaleas

Exit Road

Parking

Domestic Group

Rose S...

Britt Gro...

Hardwood Trees

Red Spruce Grove

Spruce

Spruce

Vegetable Garden

Wood Shed

Carpenter Shop

Garage Tools

Pine

Parking

Autumn Color Group

Frames

Pot Shed

Potting Shed

Green House

Garage House

Frames

Spruce & Hemlock Grove

Nursery Beds

Hemlock

Garage

Cedar

Spruce

Pine

Pine

Mountain Laurel

Spruce

Vegetable Garden & Orchard

Entrance Road

Spruce

Compost

Hemlocks

Path

Hancock Street

lowed by herbaceous and tree peonies of various old-fashioned sorts, together with St. Bruno's lily, Dane's Blood campanulas, tall sea lavenders and some of the creepers supposed to be tender in this latitude. The Chinese Jasminum nudiflorum often flowers on mild winter days and in early spring the Himalayan clematis (montana) surrounds the south window with a pinkish white wreath. Later in the season, the hybrid clematis Nelly Moser and Henryi show their flowers, followed by other clematis species such as vitalba, viticella and virginiana.

If the visitor will take a side glance at the roses on the east terrace he should nevertheless pursue his way relentlessly down the steps in order to see closely the various heathers (Callunas) in their many sorts—pink, lavender, white, and double and single; and the heaths (Ericas) the near relations of the heathers in their sundry species and varieties. These two plantations north and south of the straight walk from the southeast steps are in bloom from the end of March, when the winter heath starts the procession, until the end of September when the latest to bloom finally turn from pink and lavender to maroon and brown. At the end of the main heather plantation a narrow sunken walk diverges to the left toward a coppice woodland of small white birches and wild cherries and plums. Here the walk again turns leftward toward the house, passing a small plantation of genistas and other brooms on the right and a group of deep salmon red Kaempferi azaleas on the left. These azaleas are at their best in early and mid June, but they are followed by the splendid colouring of a few enkianthus planted among them to give autumn brilliance.

A further left turn leads up an easy slope to the single rose group on the east terrace. This collection is worthy of study as it is reported by other botanic gardens to be one of the most complete. There are various shades from pure glistening white to deep maroon red, and when their flowers are looked at with attention the purity of colour and elegance of outline will make many an observer agree with the distinguished Director of Kew Gardens, whose preference for the simplicity and perfection of line of single roses far outweighs his liking for the exuberance and size of many of the double sorts.

Finally a turn to the right will bring the visitor back to the southwest porch of the house and thence he may wish to walk up the drive to Hancock Street and see the mountain laurels and Caucasian rhododendrons when they are in bloom in June and July, or he may rejoin his parked car and drive over the same road.

If ardent garden lovers wish to make further acquaintance with plants, many little pathways will lead them through the grounds among groups of native and alien wildflowers and small rhododendrons from the ends of the earth and from the high mountains of this New England.

The gardens at Reef Point are offered to garden and plant lovers in the hope they will glean some of the pleasure it has given the first owners for over fifty years.

August 1950   BEATRIX FARRAND

THE GARDEN MONTH BY MONTH

MARCH

Snowdrops, early iris, winter aconite.

APRIL

Early bulbs, glory of the snow, scilla sibirica, crocus, early heaths and witchhazels, red maple flower.

MAY

Primroses, daffodils in the hardwood grove and under the east terrace; early lavender azaleas and prunus blossoms and sugar pears. Early perennials, dwarf apple tree bloom in the garden.

JUNE

Tulips and peonies on the terrace, English bluebells in shade plantations, woodland flowers—as twinleaf, mayapple; early azaleas—pink and white, yellows and orange in late June.

JULY

Single roses on east terrace; astilbes and other perennials in garden; climbing hydrangea and tripterygium and hybrid clematis on the house walls, and also species clematis.

AUGUST

East of house heathers and heaths: goldenrods, boneset, Joe Pyeweed and asters in bog; start of change of leaf in red maples.

SEPTEMBER

Leaf colouring growing more intense as month progresses, late aconites in garden and late sunflowers. Autumn colour plantations near north Garden Club House.

OCTOBER

Chrysanthemums in cutting garden, oaks browning to russet, crabapple fruits, burning bush (Euonymus alatus) winterberry scarlets.

NOVEMBER

Last witchhazels flowering, perhaps a few flowers on the Chinese Jasmine on the south side of the house.

George Grady Press, New York

REEF POINT GARDENS BULLETIN

Copyright, 1951, By Reef Point Gardens Corporation

PUBLISHED BY THE MAX FARRAND MEMORIAL FUND

BAR HARBOR · MAINE

Vol. I No. 7 *AUGUST*, 1951 Price 10 cents

Sewall Brown, *Photographer*

HERBARIUM CASES

Reef Point Gardens Herbarium

A STANDARD dictionary defines the word herbarium as "A collection of dried plants scientifically arranged. . . ." A distinguished botanist friend suggested, since one of the aims of Reef Point Gardens is to give opportunity for study of gardening and plant material, that an herbarium was necessary. At first the idea seemed overwhelming, but with the kindly assistance of many in the Botany Department of the University of Maine at Orono the new project was started. After the friend's helpful and stimulating suggestion was digested the necessary equipment was assembled and certain fundamental techniques studied. A small plan of the grounds was drawn on a label for the sheets of dried plant specimens, and on each label the date of collection noted. The position where the type plant was collected is indicated by a red dot, a section number given, and the correct name of the plant according to the best references. This label is essential to the student who wishes to study a particular plant after having examined the specimen on the herbarium sheet. The Engler and Prantl system is used for filing, as recommended by botanical advisers.

Due to the kindly help of several distinguished institutions the specimens now in the cases have been checked at the Arnold Arboretum for trees and shrubs, the Bailey Hortorium at Cornell for garden plants, the Royal Botanic Garden in Edinburgh for heathers and heaths, and the University of Maine for ferns and native plants. Twelve hundred specimens have been collected and pressed, and when all the woody, climbing, herbaceous, bulbous, annual, grasses and other plants have been collected the herbarium will contain nearly two thousand mounted specimens of material gathered within the six acres of Reef Point Gardens.

The plant collector should choose the proper time and select typical specimens, bearing in mind their size and future placing on the finished sheets. The red dot on each sheet label will lead the student to the identical plant from which the specimen has been taken.

Records of plant locations are being started on a system of sections for the whole acreage, and botanical and common names given, as well as the herbarium number of the plant from which the dried specimen has been collected. In addition there will be an alphabetically arranged plant material card file covering detailed information which may be of interest. This file will refer to the section and herbarium number of the individual plant and the family to which it belongs. The herbarium should be an asset to students of plant material and should so help the educational aim of the whole.

Accurate information, for which Reef Point strives, is necessary as every student of gardening or horticulture should demand high standards rather than those of mediocre calibre.

MARION IDA SPAULDING

August 1951

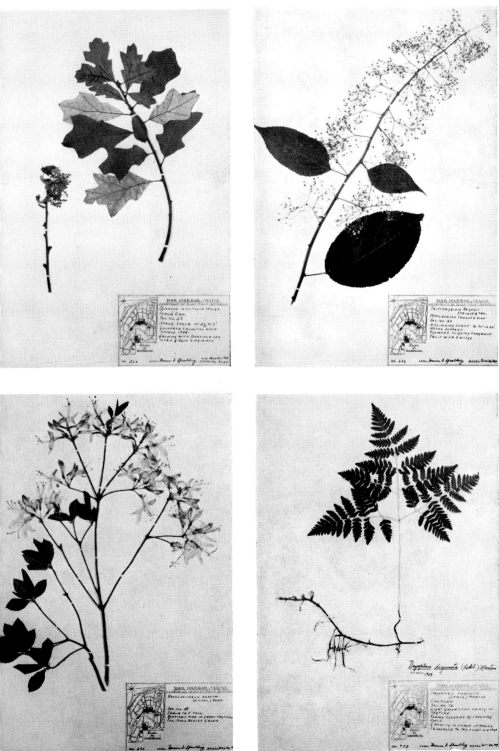

Sewall Brown, *Photographer*

COLLECTED AND PRESSED BY MARION IDA SPAULDING

THE REEF POINT GARDENS CORPORATION
Bar Harbor, Maine

OFFICERS
BEATRIX FARRAND, *President*
ALBERT HALL CUNNINGHAM, *Treasurer*
ISABELLE MARSHALL STOVER, *Clerk*

Consultant
ROBERT WHITELEY PATTERSON

Horticulturist
AMY MAGDALENE GARLAND

Recorder
MARION IDA SPAULDING

Directors
ALBERT HALL CUNNINGHAM
BEATRIX FARRAND
AGNES MILLIKEN
LAWRENCE MORRIS
CHARLES KENNETH SAVAGE
EDWIN RAY SMITH

Members

ALBERT HALL CUNNINGHAM
BEATRIX FARRAND
FAY HYLAND
LOUIS T. IBBOTSON
SUSAN DELANO MCKELVEY
AGNES MILLIKEN

LAWRENCE MORRIS
JOSEPH MAGEE MURRAY
ROBERT WHITELEY PATTERSON
CHARLES KENNETH SAVAGE
EDWIN RAY SMITH
ISABELLE MARSHALL STOVER

George Grady Press, New York

REEF POINT GARDENS BULLETIN

Copyright, 1952, by Reef Point Gardens Corporation

PUBLISHED BY THE MAX FARRAND MEMORIAL FUND

BAR HARBOR · MAINE

| Vol. I, No. 8 | *JUNE*, 1952 | Price 10 cents |

SEWALL BROWN, PHOTOGRAPHER

TALL AND DWARF WHITE SPRUCES

Conifers at Reef Point Gardens

THE cool, moist climate of the Acadian region, its thin, gravelly soils and peaty bogs are particularly suited to certain members of the conifer family, and the ledgy shores of eastern Maine and New Brunswick are fringed with spruce and pine. Mount Desert Island typifies the region, and at Reef Point the spruce skyline is the key note from the aesthetic and practical points of view.

The hills behind Bar Harbor soften the prevailing southwesterly winds, but Reef Point faces east toward Frenchman's Bay, not southward toward the open sea. It lies directly on the shore, exposed to winds in the eastern quadrants. Severe storms commonly come from these points of the compass, and with winter temperatures ranging as low as twenty degrees below zero, effective windbreaks are needed. Thick plantations of white and red spruce are accordingly called upon to bear the attack along the north and south boundaries of the property, the white spruce (Picea glauca) predominating on the easterly seaward side because of its tolerance of salt spray. The needles of this tree are a bluer green near the sea than inland, although not approaching the harsher color of P. pungens Kosteriana. Both Picea glauca and Picea rubens were growing at Reef Point when the parents of the present owner bought the land seventy years ago, and ranks of forty to sixty foot trees were fortunately standing along the north and west boundaries of the Musgrave property when its acres were added to Reef Point in 1939. On the eastern shore a few tall white spruces break the flat line of Schoodic Peninsula six miles across the bay, and between them and the house a large red spruce still survives. It is thought to be over 250 years old.

Close to the building at the northeast another white spruce group begins, and the passage from the house to the Garden Club House runs between the trunks of these tall trees. This colony forms a high secondary barrier against the northeast winds, and under its shelter are growing broad-leaved evergreens which prefer a cool northerly exposure. This plantation crosses the drive south of the parking spaces, and runs in an irregular band toward the vegetable garden. In this group white pines (Pinus strobus) are mixed with spruces, and under their high branches, on either side of the drive, are plantations of Kalmia latifolia.

Many of the large conifers at Reef Point have grown in clumps or groups, and have accordingly lost their lower branches as is usual in typical forest growth. A few, however, have been allowed to develop as more or less isolated specimens. The red spruce east of the house is one of these, and just south of this old tree is a white pine whose wide-spreading low branches shelter a thick growth of bunchberry. At the end of the principal approach from the house to the garden, a large white spruce still has its lower branches, which sweep the ground in a circle over thirty feet in diameter. This tree and the free-standing red spruce are unusual in keeping their youthful outlines, because these species under natural conditions seldom grow singly.

A fine specimen of the American arbor-vitae (Thuya occidentalis) grows near the round office on the east, but the usefulness of this tree is better shown in the clump west of the house. The drive encloses a small space opposite the front door, and within this boundary the arbor-vitaes make a dense screen which gives privacy without obstructing the road. East of the vegetable garden an equally effective group is made by hemlocks of varied species which screen the neighboring property to the south, and make a dark background for rhododendrons.

The tall spruce accents which break the flat easterly horizon are repeated in miniature near the house by so-called dwarf members of the same family. The foreground of the view is kept low, but at the edge of the lawn the entrance to three paths which lead through the heathers, to the flower garden, and to the shore, are marked by pairs of dwarf Alberta spruce (Picea glauca conica). These trees have been in their present positions for many years and are well over eight feet high, showing that dwarf is a relative term.

Another alien conifer which is frequently classified in nursery catalogues among the dwarf evergreens is the yew which grows south of the east lawn. This single plant of Taxus cuspidata densa, although only three or four feet high, covers an area over thirty feet in diameter. This Japanese yew is an unusually large specimen, but it demonstrates the fact that care must be used in choosing conifers for restricted spaces.

Certain conifers usually classed among the less desirable sorts have found places at Reef Point where they not only enjoy life but add to the picturesqueness of the composition. Pitch pine (P. rigida) is fond of the sea, Jack Pine (P. banksiana) is a hardy northerner, and both are to be found in the plantations together with red or Norway pine (P. resinosa). Deciduous conifers are not usual, but both American and European larches thrive, and Metasequoia glyptostroboides, also deciduous, is being tried in different situations, with the fingers of the gardeners crossed in the hope it will survive.

There are few coniferous trees foreign to the Island or its neighborhood which are worth planting. Forty or fifty years ago it was the fashion to think that any tree not growing locally must be better than the familiar ones. Of the many introduced trees few remain, but certain outlanders have survived and are presentable, though not as good as our own. The Scots pine (P. sylvestris) and the Austrian (P. nigra), the Douglas fir (Pseudotsuga taxifolia) and the Norway spruce (Picea abies) are the best of the immigrants. They are pleasant when young, like some human beings, but as they age, they do it without grace or dignity.

The character and colour of the Acadian landscape is given by the dominant masses of conifers, and in summer as well as in winter they add strength and beauty to the garden.

June, 1952   ROBERT WHITELEY PATTERSON

THE REEF POINT GARDENS CORPORATION
Bar Harbor, Maine

OFFICERS

BEATRIX FARRAND, *President*
ROBERT WHITELEY PATTERSON, *Vice President*
ALBERT HALL CUNNINGHAM, *Treasurer*
ISABELLE MARSHALL STOVER, *Clerk*

Consultant

ROBERT WHITELEY PATTERSON

Horticulturist

AMY MAGDALENE GARLAND

Directors

ALBERT HALL CUNNINGHAM	LAWRENCE MORRIS
BEATRIX FARRAND	ROBERT WHITELEY PATTERSON
AGNES MILLIKEN	CHARLES KENNETH SAVAGE
EDWIN RAY SMITH	

Members

ALBERT HALL CUNNINGHAM	ROGER MILLIKEN
BEATRIX FARRAND	LAWRENCE MORRIS
AMY MAGDALENE GARLAND	JOSEPH MAGEE MURRAY
FAY HYLAND	ROBERT WHITELEY PATTERSON
LOUIS T. IBBOTSON	CHARLES KENNETH SAVAGE
SUSAN DELANO MCKELVEY	EDWIN RAY SMITH
AGNES MILLIKEN	ISABELLE MARSHALL STOVER

George Grady Press, New York

REEF POINT GARDENS BULLETIN

PUBLISHED BY THE MAX FARRAND MEMORIAL FUND

BAR HARBOR · MAINE

Vol. I, No. 9   JANUARY, 1953   Price 10 cents

SEWALL BROWN, PHOTOGRAPHER

A TIDY TERRACE

45

MAINTENANCE

GOOD gardening consists in far more than setting plants in the soil. One of the best gardeners of the last three score years said "It is thoroughness, thoroughness, thoroughness that I preach. The cheapest and best of investments,—the gardener's richest capital." Reginald Farrer wrote these words and as he was acknowledged as one of the most careful and skillful horticulturists as well as a delightful writer, his opinion should be kept in mind.

Maintenance begins before even a root is planted. First, proper tools must be chosen and of good quality: a well tempered steel trowel is indispensable and the same standard should be upheld in choosing rakes, spades, shovels, hoes, weeders and mowing machinery. Second-rate and poor tools are extravagant purchases as they go to pieces, break or wear out under steady work. Once bought, tools must be kept in good condition, they should be cleaned before they are put away after the day's work, and when needed they should be sharpened. The old saying is still true in every gardener's day: "A bad reaper never found a good hook," but a bad gardener may ruin good tools by neglect and carelessness.

Stakes of the correct sizes should be in hand and clean when needed, tied in bundles of about the same size and rid of soil before they go to their winter rest. These preliminaries are necessary if proper care is to be given to plantations, large or small.

Neither does maintenance consist merely in raking roads and trimming grass verges, but it should mean constant vigilance and oversight of the plants growing in the gardener's orbit. Lawns should be fed and weeded and mown carefully, not in wavy untidy stripes with tufts of grass between the rows. Trees must be sprayed if their enemies are having a temporary victory and they also must be given nourishment. The pruning of shrubs should be made after a careful study and the season correctly chosen when the early and late flowering sorts are best trimmed. A well trimmed shrub is as much a gauge of the gardener's skill and observation as growing the most difficult rock plants. The form of each shrub should be studied so that the art of pruning is not perceptible to the ordinary garden visitor. Occasionally drastic measures are needed as may happen when an old decrepit shrub needs rejuvenating—in this case it will possibly mean reduction of the shrub overall, so that vigorous young sprouts may push forth from the tired old stumps.

Herbaceous plants must be watched as there are some that outstay their welcome and spread and lie down on more desirable and delicate neighbours. The times for division and replanting of perennials should be noted, and beds well prepared for the smaller divisions which are made from the old and woody plants.

Annuals should be started so that they may take their places as reinforcements to the early flowery perennials. It is a mistake to have large plants to set out in the early season, as they are long past their prime when they are most needed to fill the ranks of the flagging perennials in midsummer.

Watering must be done with kindness and understanding and not in the manner of an amateur cloudburst. The roots should be well and deeply moistened without drenching the foliage and inducing mildew and other wickedness lying in wait for the unskillful hand. In the season's care of the garden, not only dead flowers must be disposed of but unhealthy leaves should be taken from the plant so that tidiness and order should be subtly apparent to even a hasty visitor.

Staking must be done neither too early nor too late. Too early staking turns a garden into a forest of bare sticks or long brush far outstripping the plants they are supposed to accompany. Late staking is even worse because a strong and unexpected wind after a heavy shower may result in flattened colonies of delphinium or bent lily stems or even uprooting of plants lightly held in the garden soil.

Each garden composition must be studied as a whole, and the balance of the original planter or designer kept in mind. Sometimes perennials grow far beyond what they are intended to do, and balance must be restored if the composition is to remain a true picture.

Good weeding consists in taking the offender out literally root and branch, making sure the last, least, wicked and unwanted root is taken out with as little injury to the soil and surroundings as possible. The easy weeding method is to chop off the heads of the intruders, leaving their thriving roots eager to recommence their invasion. The chemical weed killers may be useful in many instances, but there may be risk in using them through consequent injury to a nearby cherished plant.

There should be changes made in the garden from time to time in order to keep the original composition from getting out of balance. One garden was repeated year after year precisely as originally planted with the result that a mechanical series of groups was slavishly followed and the garden became a repeated pattern like a wall paper.

It is as useless to try to make plants grow where their likings are not consulted as it would be to plant seaweed in a desert, therefore each and every plant, tree or shrub must be studied; the soil it best likes, the exposures to light and shade that are favourable, and where wind and dryness would lead to disappointment and disaster. In short, if eternal vigilance is the price of peace, maintenance and watchfulness are the price of good gardening.

Francis Bacon's words written long ago are still true

> "God Almighty first planted a garden; and indeed it is the
> purest of human pleasures—"

But it must be a good garden not a weedy unkempt one; as gardens are living things and need observation, care and affection.

AMY MAGDALENE GARLAND

January 1953

George Grady Press, New York

REEF POINT GARDENS BULLETIN

Copyright, 1953, by Reef Point Gardens Corporation

PUBLISHED BY THE MAX FARRAND MEMORIAL FUND

BAR HARBOR · MAINE

Vol. I, No. 10   *JUNE*, 1953   Price 10 cents

Sewall Brown, Photographer

HYBRID TEA ROSE INNOCENCE

49

Single and Semi-double Roses

THE PAGES of early Books of Hours are often surrounded by little flowers strewn on a burnished gold background. Doubtless one who has been fortunate enough to hold one of these precious leaves in his hands will remember that most of the flowers are single. Artists in the middle ages and the early Renaissance seemed to feel beauty in purity of line, and the simple contours of the petals were more to their liking than the double flowers which later became the fashion with Dutch and Italian painters. The violets and lilies of Leonardo's drawings, the columbines and celandines under Durer's master hand may be seen on their sketch sheets and they have remained through the years as the most complete and perfect expression of beauty in single flowers.

The collection of single roses at Reef Point Gardens has grown from one or two to over twenty different sorts. It is now said to be the most complete group of single hybrid tea roses either in this country or abroad, and certain kinds are only to be seen at Reef Point. Among these are the beautiful spinel coloured Armstrong Ruby; the delicate pink with red brown anthers of Ellen Willmott; the deeper pink Ethel James with yellow centre. Sweet Sue is a madder rose dark centred kind and Colette Clement is cherry colour, sweet scented with yellow centre and almost semi-double. All of these are fragrant and last well when cut for the house.

Many nurserymen have repeatedly told those in charge of the rose terrace that single roses are not in fashion and that they therefore no longer list them in their catalogues. In days past the following singles and semi-doubles were obtainable, but nowadays Irish Beauty and Irish Elegance have been almost lost to cultivation, as well as Ethel James, Ellen Willmott and La Nigrette. Dainty Bess remains in an occasional catalogue rather apologetically added at the foot of lists emphasizing large size and quantities of petals.

Few visitors to the Gardens fail to remark on the beauty and vigour of the plants on the rose terrace. There are not more than a hundred plants, but every day from mid-June to late October one or other is in bloom.

The hard work of the rose bulletin has been done by the two colleagues who have painstakingly cared for, and thoroughly studied, compared and measured, the rose blooms throughout a season. The sizes, shades, character, and strength of growth have been noted and the accompanying lists and charts are the result of close observation and accurate notes.

BEATRIX FARRAND

Look to the rose that blows about us —"Lo
Laughing," she says, "into the world I blow."

The Care of Single Roses

There is no especial magic needed for the care of either single or double roses. The main requirement is constant observation of their needs. Watering should be carefully done so that leaves are not drenched and left wet over night. Sickly leaves should at once be picked off the bush and put into a bag for later burning, so that black spot and other evil fungus be not allowed to fall on the ground and so spread spores to infect healthy plants. The winter protection in eastern Maine must be carefully done after hard frosts deaden the ground. A hilling up of eight or ten inches of soil around each bush, plus a cover of spruce boughs are a part of the season's routine. Added to these routines should be a weekly stirring or light cultivating of the soil, and a weekly spraying against the attacks of fungus or insect enemies. Fertilizing is done with old cow manure and bone meal, and hardwood ashes in April. Then in late May, or very early June, a trowelful of a complete commercial fertilizer such as 5–8–7 is given to each plant.

Amy Magdalene Garland

The Charts

It is no more possible to describe a rose than to reduce to words the light in a Vermeer, and the chart shown on the center pages of this bulletin is only an attempt to define a few characteristics of the best of the Reef Point roses. It might be expected that quite accurate definitions could be made by using such excellent colour charts as those of the Royal Horticultural Society, but even here there is nothing with which to compare the delicate shading, the texture, and the indescribably soft, almost luminous quality of the rose colours. By flattening a petal on the charts it was possible to make reasonably accurate definitions, but only when the play of light was reduced by masking with black paper so that only a small part of the petal and the printed colour were visible.

Average representative flowers, freshly opened, were selected for study and definition, and the measurements and colours were taken from these individual blooms. The length of stamens varies considerably, and the measurement given is the average length of the stamens on the bloom selected for study. The type and number of petals was determined by study of several specimens, and the remarks under "Comments" and "Character of Bush" are the result of observation of all the plants of each species.

There is more or less variation in both size and colour even among flowers on the same plant, and colours often change noticeably after the first day. It cannot therefore be expected that they will be in all cases exactly as recorded here; but the charts may be useful as a record of the principal features of fresh blooms produced on healthy and well-grown plants in the climate of coastal Maine.

Robert Whiteley Patterson

THE TWENTY BEST ROSES AT REEF POINT GARDENS

The names and numbers of colours are taken from "Horticultural Colour Chart," Charts I and II issued by The British Colour Council in collaboration with The Royal Horticultural Society

NAME	DIAMETER OF BLOOM	PETALS Type and Number	PETALS Colour
Ami Quinard	4"	Semi-double	828 Garnet La
Armstrong Ruby No. 40080–8	3½"–4"	5–6 Ends variously scalloped.	724 Rose Red
Armstrong Seedling No. 41160–8	6"	Semi-double. Long, narrow, recurved.	3 Aureolin center. Outer two thirds 622 Camellia Rose. Backs pale in both colors, more yello than pink.
Cecil	4½"	5	2/2 Canary Yellow
Colette Clément	3½"	Semi-double	722/3 Cherry. 4/1 Lemon Yellow center, sm
Dainty Bess	3¾"	5	523/1 Dawn Pink
Ellen Willmott	4½"	5–6	White. 527/1 Rhodamin Pink tips.
Ethel James	3¼"	5	25/2 Rose Bengal. 2/2 Canary Yellow center.
Innocence	4½"	6–7	White. Edge of petals tinged with 629/2 Roseine Purple.

		STAMENS		
h	*Colour*	*Colour of Anthers*	CHARACTER OF BUSH	COMMENTS
	628/3 Persian Rose	Brown	Strong.	Fragrant.
ed	07/1 Yellow Ochre	Dark ochreish brown (no match).	Strong, foliage good.	Fragrant. Petals rather loose.
" ed.	07/1 Yellow Ochre	09 Majolica Yellow	Strong, foliage good.	Very fragrant. Stamens hidden. Back of center petals visible. Does not last well when cut.
	4/1 Lemon Yellow	Brown	Fairly strong.	Flat, slightly recurved.
'	6/1 Indian Yellow	6/2 Indian Yellow	Strong, good foliage.	Fragrant.
	727 Tyrian Purple	Dark ochre	Strong.	Flat, open bloom.
	24/2 Tyrian Rose	Reddish brown	Strong.	Fragrant. Flat, cup-shaped bloom.
"	2/1 Canary Yellow	07/1 Yellow Ochre	Strong.	Fragrant.
	822/1 Cardinal Red	Dark ochre	Strong.	Flat, open bloom.

53

NAME	DIAMETER OF BLOOM	PETALS	
		Type and Number	*Colour*
Irish Beauty	3¾″	6	White
Irish Elegance	3¼″	5	2/2 Canary Yellow center, shading to 22/3 Crimson.
Irish Fireflame	3½″–4″	5	2/1 Canary Yellow center, to 4/3 Lemon Yellow, to 20/2 Geranium Lake.
Isobel	4″	5	724/3 Rose Red. 3/1 Aureolin center.
Kitchener of Khartoum	4″	Semi-double	724 Rose Red, dark.
La Nigrette	3¼″	5–6	1030 Maroon
Memory	4″	Semi-double	24/3 Tyrian Rose
Simplicity	3″–3½″	8, plus 1 or more small and imperfect.	White, with very faint yellow tinge in center.
Sweet Sue	4″	5–6 Rather long, slightly recurved.	23/1 Rose Madder, shading to small very pale yellowish center.
Vesuvius	3½″	5	824 Chrysanthemum Crimson
White Wings	5½″	5–6	White. Tips very faintly tinged with 24/3 Tyrian Rose.

th	Colour	Colour of Anthers	CHARACTER OF BUSH	COMMENTS
	2/3 Canary Yellow	07/1 Yellow Ochre	Fairly strong.	Fragrant.
	3/1 Aureolin	07/1 Yellow Ochre	Fairly strong.	Fragrant. Pale yellow center shading to pale rose. Open.
" tly ed.	4/1 Lemon Yellow	6/1 Indian Yellow	Rather weak.	Fragrant. General effect: single, recurved, pale ochre-ish center shading to Rose edges. Lasts fairly well when cut.
	07 Yellow Ochre	Medium ochre	Fairly strong.	Flat, open bloom.
	26/2 Solferino Purple	Brown	Fairly strong.	
	28/1 Dianthus Purple	Brown	Rather weak.	
	24/3 Tyrian Rose	07/1 Yellow Ochre	Strong.	Fairly fragrant. Rather curly.
tly ed	2/2 Canary Yellow	7/2 Saffron Yellow	Strong.	Fragrant, small cup-shaped bloom.
	022/1 Rose Opal	Dark ochre-ish brown (no match).	Strong, good foliage.	Slightly fragrant, petals long, convex.
	28/1 Dianthus Purple	Medium ochre	Weak.	Flat, very slightly recurved.
	025 Spiraea Red	09/2 Majolica Yellow	Rather weak.	Fragrant.

55

George Grady Press, New York

REEF POINT GARDENS BULLETIN

Copyright, 1954, by Reef Point Gardens Corporation

PUBLISHED BY THE MAX FARRAND MEMORIAL FUND

BAR HARBOR · MAINE

Vol. I, No. 11   *JUNE*, 1954   Price 10 cents

Sewall Brown, Photographer

CLIMBING HYDRANGEA

Climbing Plants in Eastern Maine

THE TWO papers written for the Brooklyn Botanic Garden's "Plants & Gardens" are reprinted by courtesy of the Director and the Editor. As several changes were made in the manuscript the original wording has been restored by the two writers.

Twenty years ago the seed of an idea for Reef Point Gardens germinated in the minds of Max and Beatrix Farrand. As they had enjoyed their house and garden for twenty or more years, they began from that time to plan for its future as a guide, companion and helper to garden lovers and students of gardening. About eight years ago Beatrix Farrand started the actual redesigning of the house and grounds, as a memorial to her husband and their love of gardening in eastern Maine. They had often spoken of a wish to show climbing plants in a becoming and horticulturally correct way, and with this goal in view the house and galleries connected to two nearby garden houses were reconstructed or built anew. The result is that over six hundred feet of wall space is now given to the cultivation of climbers of various sorts which have already proven themselves hardy in cold winters and patient of dry and sometimes hot days. Others have been added; and many of these should be included in the delightfully expressive phrase "precariously hardy," but they seem to enjoy themselves year after year about three hundred feet from the shore of Frenchman's Bay.

A complete collection of climbers was clearly out of the question, consequently those of comparatively easy culture and recognized attractiveness were first chosen. One of the very first to be planted over seventy years ago were two Dutchman's pipes (Aristolochia durior) which were set on either side of the entrance porch, where they still flourish. Perhaps the leaves are a trifle coarse and large in scale, but they have been in their places so long that a hard heart would be needed to uproot them. The old Virginia Creeper (Parthenocissus quinquefolia) was also planted when the house was built, but only scraps of this remain, as they have been pulled out, crowded unmercifully, and ruthlessly cut back. The more finely leaved P. quinquefolia Engelmannii grows well and is not as overwhelmingly invasive as its larger cousin. Of course the so-called Boston Ivy, (P. tricuspidata) is represented but is not allowed to ramp and cover the buildings like a glove,—it is kept carefully pruned so that only the finer shoots cling to the low stone wall where it is planted. The blue berried Ampelopsis brevipedunculata is lovely in the autumn and drapes itself in hanging garlands over a small garage. The true grapes are represented by Vitis Thunbergii from China and V. riparia of our own eastern states. A splendid plant of Vitis Coignetiae was growing vigorously on the south side of the main house and its great leaves were gorgeous in colour every autumn. A large established plant, it was moved unwisely, as it grew directly in the path of the remodelling. It sulked and finally died, but one of these days a successor will be planted to gladden the eyes of autumn visitors. Edible grapes are also planted on the solid fences surrounding the vegetable garden.

Although the Farrands were plant lovers they realized they should not attempt anything approaching a complete assemblage of climbers, and they therefore deliberately limited themselves to choosing two or three of their favourite sorts to grow in a representative collection. The two predominant kinds selected were clematis and honeysuckles. These were at first tried tentatively, and in finding that the first trials were surprisingly successful the numbers of species, varieties and hybrids were increased. Some were planted with little hope of success, but many of these grew well and withstood temperature changes of over a hundred degrees, as occasional winter nights push the thermometer down to fifteen or twenty degrees below zero, and hot summer suns can stimulate the mercury to over ninety.

The honeysuckles were known to be fairly hardy as the porches of old cottages on the Island were draped with the climbing shoots and red flowers of Lonicera sempervirens. Therefore it was planted, but the Reef Point specimen is rather sulky, because the right place has not yet been found for it. Then the English Woodbine, (Lonicera Periclymenum) was timorously tried and responded with unbounded enthusiasm. A low wall supporting the little rose terrace is fragrant with its flowers almost all summer and its glistening red berries are attractively borne with the late season flowers; the variety belgica is also grown. The early blooming L. Caprifolium is also a joy as the fragrant blooms in the early season are both astonishing and pleasing. Within the last few years L. Caprifolium has had troubles, perhaps fungus of some sort not yet known at Reef Point Gardens or perhaps a virulent mildew. But it is a beautiful climber and the colour and vigour of the flowers and leaves are refreshing. Lonicera tragophylla from China was given to the gardens by the Arnold Arboretum and for some years was spectacular with its large butter yellow heads of flowers and bronzish green leaves; this sort has been a little unhappy lately, although perfectly hardy. Its child, L. x Tellmanniana, a cross between L. tragophylla and L. sempervirens, is more gorgeous in its orange colour, but it too has had attacks of illness and though also quite hardy has shown signs of misery and one plant, on a neighbour's place, just suddenly "up and died" in midsummer. A horticultural clinic is needed for these three sorts, as they are too ornamental and fragrant to lose without a struggle. The inconspicuous flowers of L. flava, and its beautiful foliage decorate an iron railing on eastward-facing steps, and L. Heckrottii seems quite contented both on the east and west sides of the northern garden house. The pestilently invasive L. japonica is fortunately not hardy, but the others are strong and attractive, and add greatly to the many walls of the house. In fact, many of the honeysuckles are happier in eastern Maine than in the hotter summers of southern New England and the Middle Atlantic states. And they are less troubled by aphis invasion.

Professor Charles Sprague Sargent, first Director of the Arnold Arboretum was endlessly kind to his pupil Mrs. Farrand, and often gave her surplus plants to try in the more dramatic climate of eastern Maine. One bundle contained a Tripterygium Regelii which Professor Sargent scornfully described as a "dud," to which Reef Point was most welcome as the Arboretum could not make it happy. This species of the Celastrus family was planted on the southeast corner of the house, and started to grow with rampant cheerfulness. Its sweetly scented trusses of tiny flowers are often

TRUSS OF TRIPTERYGIUM

nearly three feet in length, and in July the whole side of the house is as murmurous with bees as any English lime tree walk. It comes from the mountains of eastern Asia, and apparently rejoices in the cold climate of Bar Harbor. It is clean and very strong in growth and thrives so well that its seeds have been distributed to many botanic and private gardens. In fact tripterygium is treated as a stop-gap and generally useful plant. Where an architectural utility is particularly evident, a "Trip" is planted and soon races up an ugly downspout or floats its long streamers from an awkward corner. The one thing the "Trips" will not stand is lack of water—they need copious draughts of it even when their neighbours show no signs of flagging. Of course the relatives of tripterygium, Celastrus scandens (Bittersweet) and the Asiatic C. orbiculatus are grown with success.

Before starting the long list of clematis, a few scattered climbers may be mentioned. The "utility" class should include Actinidia arguta, as it is iron clad hardy and as free from disease and insect pests as tripterygium. Actinidias are clean and fresh all summer and toward autumn bear a green fruit, which looks indigestible, but is said to be pleasant and mild in flavor. Akebia is always attractive as its foliage is clean of insects, somewhat greyish green in colour and in early summer the clusters of mulberry coloured little flowers hide under the leaves and twining and waving ends of the branches. Akebia quinata is a staunch standby and grows freely yet gracefully on any of the four compass point exposures. The Baltic Ivy (Hedera helix baltica) is happiest when overgrown by another climber.

On the west side of the house it snuggles under a light and flowery mass of late flowering yellow clematis, and tightly clings to an old brick chimney apparently accepting with complaisance the matted growth of a big climbing hydrangea. At one time Wisteria sinensis was grown on the south side of the house, but finally it was dismissed as it was agreed that "its room was better than its company". To be sure it grew well and the healthy leaves were pretty, but it flowered sparsely and the waving branches were a nuisance to train and keep in bounds, and furthermore it took up space now occupied by clematis and honeysuckle. Euonymus Fortunei var. vegeta is a singleton grown at the foot of a low wall, and vigorously pruned so that it is often mistaken for a shrub. This plant attracts scale like a magnet, and although the plant is still clean of this pest, it is troublesome to keep in bounds and in good order, so only one specimen is grown. It must be acknowledged that its lustrous evergreen leaves and orange red fruit are attractive when all the other creepers have shed their leaves for their winter sleep.

The two plants which make the most spectacular show in late June and early July are the Tripterygium with its long plumes of creamy green flowers, and the two big Hydrangea petiolaris, one on the east and one on the west side of the house. Each one is thirty or more feet high with hundreds of soft white flowers and sturdy red twigs, held well out from the wall. It is a joy to see these two creepers full of strength and life, and clinging so firmly to boards, shingles, plaster or stone that no laborious tying is needed. Sometimes after a particularly cruel winter the hydrangea seems to resent the cold by flowering a little less freely. Its less well known cousin Schizophragma hydrangeoides has not yet attained the height and strength of the climbing hydrangea but it grows well and is hardy on the north side of the north garden house, and its flowers, somewhat like the hydrangea, have a peculiar distinction.

Probably the most generally admired climbers are the whole clematis group. They are in bloom from late May when C. montana rubens surrounds a south window with its graceful garlands. Following C. montana there is a clematis in flower until well on into October. There seems no halt in the procession, and when one ceases flowering its neighbour "takes up the wond'rous tale" until the whole summer has been beautified by their grace and charm. The south window frame on which C. montana rubens grows looks like the frontispiece to an old gardening book with its delicate reddish shoots and soft pink flowers. It is easily trained and never seems to complain, even on hot summer days. The species, rather than the hybrids of clematis have been chosen for decoration of the Reef Point walls; they are not as spectacularly effective, but are easier to grow and seem less subject to sudden ailments which shorten the lives of many of the large flowered hybrids. However, quite early in the season the hybrid Nelly Moser displays her pale lavender flowers in profusion on the east side of the south garden house. And here, in passing it may be wise to say that almost all the creepers described have east or west exposures and consequently are not forced to endure a whole day of hot sunshine. The Vitalbas are among the most faithful and trustworthy: the native C. virginiana, the European C. Vitalba (Traveler's Joy) and the western C. ligusticifolia have all been grown with ease and satisfaction. The western species needs replacement as an evil borer attacked it beyond hope of recovery. Other true species seem contented, among others, C. texensis with its attractive thick red sepals and lovely feathery seed heads. Clematis crispa and C. fusca grow well, and while somewhat unlike texensis, the flower shapes in pale lavender and white are a little like those of C. texensis. The Atragene section are attractive and vigorous and C. Viticella has made itself so at home that its seedlings sprout with determination near the parent plant. The deep violet blue flowers, while small, are carried in profusion and make a delightful wall cover. A late species is C. apiifolia, a creamy mass of bloom on an eastward-facing step balustrade. This species is strangely seldom grown, while its relative and later blooming sort, C. paniculata, is seen everywhere and is always pretty.

There are hybrids of C. Viticella,—C. Viticella kermesina, and Lady Betty Balfour, which are to be trusted as to hardiness and regular flowering, and are well worth growing. Some of the large-flowered hybrids are more coquettish and harder to please. C. Jackmanii is beginning to be satisfied now that its feet are shaded by low box bushes, but it does dislike the baking of the western sun. C. Henryi is grown, but is more contented in a neighbour's garden, but Comtesse de Bouchard is more patient and flowers fairly late in the season. Madame Edouard André, the deep red sort, is doing her best, but is not yet pleased with her position. The hybrid of C. texensis, Dutchess of Albany is a good grower and pushes its way to the top of the south garden house, with its slender shoots and deep pink flowers. The hybrid of C. heracliaefolia, C. x Jouiniana is an excellent and sturdy plant. The stiff shoots and plentiful bluish-white flowers frame the eastern library windows and the plant is ironclad hardy. Another heracliaefolia hybrid is Mrs. Robert Brydon, a deeper blue more like its parent, but less strong growing than Jouiniana.

Toward the end of the season the small yellow tulip-like pendent flowers of C. tangutica var. obtusiuscula cover the delicate shoots, and later still the seed heads fairly iridescent in the autumn afternoon sun are nearly as lovely as the flowers.

No doubt the omission of climbing roses will be noticed. Only two sorts are grown, the well known and healthy Doctor W. Van Fleet and the little known French rose Réveil Dijonnais. These two are cultivated just to show climbing roses can be grown, but many sorts are difficult, they need much spraying, or they mildew and are cantankerous about winter cold, in fact they are rather troublesome customers.

Climbing plants are cherished by those who work at Reef Point Gardens and are admired by visitors as everyone realizes that the walls they cover are made into vertical flower beds, full of charm and beauty. In fact growing climbers is one of the most rewarding and least troublesome of the many forms of garden art.

BEATRIX FARRAND

Cultivation of Climbing Plants at Reef Point Gardens

MANY of those who do their gardening in southern New England and the Middle States have an idea that eastern coastal Maine is like their own surroundings. Nothing could be less accurate, as the eastern coast of the easternmost New England counties is far more like the neighbouring province of New Brunswick in Canada. The soil is usually thin and rocks

Sewall Brown, Photographer

TRIPTERYGIUM REGELII

lie near the surface, and drainage is good except in occasional clay pockets left by glaciers. The climate is far more nearly that of nearby Canada than Connecticut or western Massachusetts. All of these natural conditions must be accepted as fundamental in any gardening effort in the seacoast region of eastern Maine.

But what riches the thin soil holds, light, clean, and friable, it gives returns to a gardener far beyond his deserts. Climbing plants which suffer in the heat of the Middle States, thrive and prosper, honeysuckles that are tormented by aphis in the warmer climates are healthy on the Island and full of flower, in fact many clematis species take kindly to the rigorous

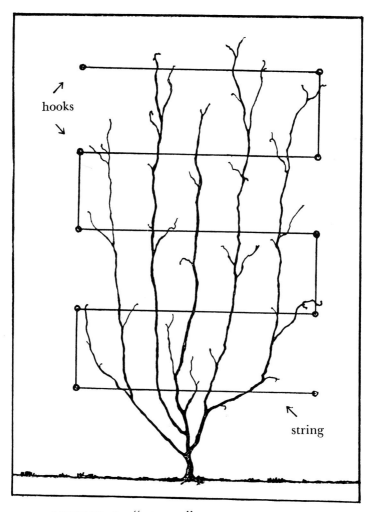

METHOD OF "LACING" A VINE TO A WALL

climate, and of course the "iron-clads" like akebia, actinidia and celastrus are enthusiastic growers.

Planting must be done with care, and preferably in the spring,—a generously sized hole with lime or lime rubble and coal ashes is used for clematis, together with a commercial fertilizer such as 5–8–7, and bone meal. For the other creepers well rotted cow manure replaces the lime and coal ashes.

Training the creepers is one of the early summer tasks which takes time and patience but is essential if the plant is to look tidy and show its flowers or growth becomingly. A simple method has been evolved after years of struggle and failure. The system is only applicable to climbers of fairly light growth, as heavy wooded plants like tripterygium, celastrus and actinidia require heavy tying with thick soft cord attached to stout nails. The clematis and honeysuckles are laced into place like the oldfashioned hunting boot. Hooks are placed in the wooden walls, or on battens for this purpose placed on stucco or plaster. These hooks are turned downwards and a long roll of soft tan string is started at the bottom and laced up to the hooks in horizontal and vertical lines, which the accompanying diagram will illustrate. In this way the growth of the creeper can be followed by extending the string to another level, where the little bunch of cord is tied and used again when another foot or so of growth needs to be led in the way in which it should go. The small flowered clematis, such as C. montana rubens or C. Viticella may be trained by this method to make a complete windowframe. The simplicity of the arrangement is manifest, and the creeper can be unlaced, laid down, or new shoots tied in with no difficulty or waste of tying material. Spraying is done occasionally with nicotine sulphate to fight aphis on the honeysuckles, but is only needed in what coastal eastern Maine calls hot weather.

The climbers mentioned in the longer article are all growing within two hundred and fifty or three hundred feet of the shores of Frenchman's Bay. They are lashed by heavy northeasters both in summer and winter, and if there is spray in the blasting winds they seem not to object to it. There has never been the "fog-burning" which is dreaded on Long Island and the southern coasts of New England. But the Bar Harbor plants do not like the hot southwest winds in midsummer and show their distress by turning leaves inside out and looking bedraggled and insulted for several days after the wind blasting is over.

It is interesting to those in charge of the Reef Point Gardens climbers to note on their inland drives how few of the sorts grown by the seaside are attempted. In fact at the University of Maine in Orono, only fifty miles inland as the traditional crow flies, where the soil is clayey and the climate truly continental rather than maritime, many of the plants decline to live. The "Trips" are very unhappy in Connecticut where they were planted on the college buildings at Yale, and some of the clematis species just frizzle up in the heat. Certain of the iron-clads like celastrus and actinidia endure the inland climate and the heat, but it is hard to dogmatise as many of the clematis species and honeysuckles do not seem to be grown elsewhere, even by enthusiastic gardeners.

Certain shrubs are used as wall plants; for example Winter Jasmine (Jasminum nudiflorum) is tucked into the most sheltered corner on the south side of the main house near Clematis montana rubens. It is given a light covering of spruce boughs, in order to protect its buds, and gratefully answers to the treatment by giving winter flowers. On warm days in December and January the golden flowers appear on the green twigs, and if cut in bud and taken into a warmish room they give the lovely promise of oncoming spring. This twig cutting is almost the only pruning needed.

Sewall Brown, Photographer

CLEMATIS NELLY MOSER

A big forsythia is trained on a less protected wall, and if allowed its own way it climbs in its string harness above a second story window. In ferocious winters the upper flower buds are blasted, but the lower ones do their spring duty where they can have even the slight protection of spruce or fir boughs. The particular forsythia is a seedling from one of the first wall plants planted on the north side of a line of college buildings at Princeton over forty years ago, where they are trained up to the eaves over the second story windows, and turn the wall into a sheet of gold in early spring.

While fruit trees are not technically climbing plants, they are treated as such, and in the shelter of the six or seven foot kitchen garden fence, peach trees are spread out and tacked on the boards in the old French palmate pattern. The trees are grateful for the wind protection of the wall and usually yield good crops of fruit.

Further training methods have been invented to meet the local circumstances, for example the English Woodbine, (Lonicera Periclymenum,) is trained on horizontal lines on the low dry stone wall which supports the eastern rose terrace. Wedge-shaped pieces of wood are hammered firmly into the crannies of the wall, and staples or nails again hammered into the flat outer ends of the wedges. Strings are tied to these anchors and the woodbine trained behind these light cords. The woodbines trained in this fashion seem to be less leggy and bare at the base than those trained perpendicularly.

Pruning is done usually in spring—the old wood of the forsythias, tripterygiums, actinidias and akebias is shortened or eliminated, where it can be done without deforming the plant by over-much slashing. Although textbooks say the clematis should be heavily pruned each spring, the species grown do not seem to ask more than judicious thinning and cleaning out of old used-up wood.

Many of the climbers growing at Reef Point Gardens are not supposed to be thoroughly hardy as far east and north, but no gardener is ever content until he experiments and perhaps fails, but more often succeeds in establishing in happy life a new and worthwhile garden inhabitant.

All who work in the gardens are trying to learn, sometimes by trial and error, sometimes in a spirit of adventure—since after all is said and done, gardening is like many other human efforts of which it may truly be said "Nothing venture nothing have—".

AMY MAGDALENE GARLAND

REEF POINT GARDENS BULLETIN

Copyright, 1954, by Reef Point Gardens Corporation

PUBLISHED BY THE MAX FARRAND MEMORIAL FUND

BAR HARBOR · MAINE

Vol. 1, No. 12   *J U L Y,* 1954   Price 10 cents

Photograph by Sargent Collier, courtesy of the Editor of *Horticulture*

GENERAL VIEW OF HEATHS AND HEATHERS

Heaths

Heaths (Ericas) and heathers (Callunas) are closely related, but when examined with attention they are noticeably different. The heaths have larger flowers than the heathers and their leaves are not so closely pressed against the stem nor so tiny. The differences can easily be seen by looking at the two centre pictures in which heaths and heathers are placed opposite each other. In general the heaths are a little less resistant to our winter climate, but both cousins require the same soil, exposure, watering and care. The ericas often start their bloom in March, and different sorts and species continue the flowery season well into September and October.

There is no need to comment on the attractiveness of the heaths, as they are among the first flowers of the spring and their delicate twigs and small bell flowers keep in water for two or three weeks. The little bushes themselves are pretty, symmetrical and yet not stiff, and the quantities of small flowers nearly hide the fine foliage. The dark anthers and pistils add to the charm of the little bells as they are a sharp contrast in colour. The bell heath, Erica Tetralix, and its varieties fascinate all visitors to Reef Point, many bent heads are noticed examining the white, pink, or deep red bells as they appear, one after another. Although visitors are not plentiful when E. carnea and its varieties open in early spring, the little branches with their gay pendant flowers brighten a room on a cold dreary spring day when out of doors the skies are lowering and the wind is still keen. The northern heaths are spread over the whole of Europe, Norway, Lapland and Scotland where they and the heathers are the dominating plants of the romantic Highland mountains. A vast majority of the heaths are, however, South African plants, as the Christmas pots of so-called heather are Erica canaliculata. Erica mediterreanea is grown in huge hedges in Italy, but we must content ourselves with the humbler low growing kinds that have been a part of Scottish literature and poetry since men began to sing and write.

Plant loving travellers who have circled the earth have repeatedly said that the most impressive and beautiful display of flowers is to be seen in August in the Scottish highlands, where heaths and heathers bloom together on mile after mile of mountainside. They are as precise in their blooming season as a standard chronometer and as August twelfth marks the opening of the grouse shooting season in Scotland, it also marks the start of the finest heather bloom.

At Reef Point an effort has been made to try and make as many of the heaths happy in the dour climate of Eastern coastal Maine as possible, and more than twenty sorts have found places in the little heath garden east of the house. The Dorset and Cornish heaths do not like cold winters too well, but they indomitably start again from the root, when a rude winter kills their tops. Even the Irish heath Daboecia survives, but with a mighty struggle to wake up again in the spring.

> " 'Tis my faith that every flower
> Enjoys the air it breathes . . . "

BEATRIX FARRAND

Erica Species and Varieties Grown
at Reef Point Gardens

Numbers refer to herbarium specimens in The Reference Library. Many have been identified at the Royal Botanic Garden, Edinburgh, Professor Sir William Wright Smith, Regius Keeper.

ERICA CARNEA, the earliest flowering heath at Reef Point, often in bloom in late March or early April. The carneas are not quite as hardy as some of the Callunas and after severe winters show some stem splitting. They almost always come up from the root even after a hard winter of changing temperatures. Colour a deep spinel ruby red. Excellent as a small cut flower in earliest spring.

ERICA CARNEA KING GEORGE, deep dark-toned rosy crimson flowers. Award of Merit, Royal Horticultural Society.

ERICA CARNEA RUBY GLOW, a fine very deep ruby colour.

ERICA CARNEA SPRINGWOOD, the white variety of this sort is one of the most attractive of the early heaths. It grows rapidly, into a small semi-trailing bush, covered with white flowers in April and May. Foliage light green.

ERICA CARNEA SPRINGWOOD PINK, many consider this the finest of the carneas, with its white cousin—Springwood.

ERICA CARNEA VIVELLI, bells a deep carmine red and foliage turns to a reddish shade in autumn.

ERICA CILIARIS (DORSET HEATH), a somewhat tender but lovely plant valuable for its flowers, larger than Tetralix and cinerea, of soft greyish pink. It has been killed to the ground several times but bravely comes back to life and flower. September, October.

ERICA CILIARIS DAWN, very like the true ciliaris but flowers slightly larger and paler.

900   ERICA CINEREA VAR. ATRORUBENS, long sprays of deep red flowers on trailing stalks, a fine sort blooming in July, August.

901   ERICA CINEREA C. D. EASON, a plant always noticed in the groups for its bright deep red flower and symmetrical bush. Flowers early in July and August.

ERICA CINEREA DOMINO, foliage dark green with dark flower stalks. Flowers plentiful and white.

1093   ERICA HYBRIDA WILLIAMSI, a cross between E. vagans and Tetralix. The growth of this plant is interesting in the whorls of four leaves on slender twigs, and small tufts of pink flowers at the stem tips give it individuality in any collection.

1014   ERICA MACKAII FLORE-PLENO, a double pink form by some authorities said to be a variety of E. Tetralix, and by others to be a distinct species. Flowers quite large and rosy pink in July and August.

1141   ERICA TETRALIX, the ordinary pink flowered form of the large bell flowered heath, blooms from late July to September.

646   ERICA TETRALIX, VAR. ALBA MOLLIS, a softly pubescent form of the well known Tetralix, a charming plant freely blooming with white bells at top of stiff little twigs and in constant flower from late July to September.

ERICA TETRALIX GEORGE FRASER, flowers pale pink and foliage has a bluish cast.

1090 ERICA VAGANS ALBA MINOR, a very dwarf form of alba, flowering in August and September.

1010 ERICA VAGANS VAR. LYONESSE, a white-flowered sort, rather more stubby in flower than the pink St. Keverne, and blooming a trifle later, a variety recognized by an Award of Merit at the Royal Horticultural Society, and well worth growing. The plant and its flowers, even though not brilliant, are attractive even into October.

939 ERICA VAGANS ST. KEVERNE, a clear pink sort with the characteristic tufted cluster of flowers at the top of the stem. A pleasant little shrub with attractive flowers blooming in late August.

DABOECIA CANTABRICA (POLIFOLIA), the so-called Irish Heath; not nearly as hardy as the Callunas or Ericas but well worth growing even if cut to the ground by cold winters. The bells are larger than most Ericas, and a deep plum red, flowering in August and September. The little bush is slenderer than the Ericas.

ERICA CINEREA
C. D. EASON

ERICA CILIARIS
DAWN

ERICA TETRALIX
WHITE AND PINK

ERICA VAGANS
ST. KEVERNE

ERICA CARNEA
SPRINGWOOD

CALLUNA VULGARIS
ALBA RIGIDA

CALLUNA VULGARIS
COUNTY WICKLOW

CALLUNA VULGARIS
HAMMONDII

CALLUNA VULGARIS
J. H. HAMILTON

CALLUNA VULGARIS
VAR. RUBRA

Heathers

THE true heathers (Callunas) are a trifle hardier than the heaths, but they have not as large flowers and in consequence they are not usually as much admired as the heaths.

The preparation and planting and care of the two closely related sorts is the same. They both need light sandy soil, full sun, perfect drainage and annual clipping either of dead flowers or of shoots that have outgrown their usefulness. In making the bed for these friendly plants a fairly generous quantity of powdery old cow manure should be incorporated with the lower layer of soil, then ground peat from the local peat bogs (not sphagnum peat moss) should be worked into the upper light soil, as the peat holds moisture and stimulates root growth. The preparation of the planting space should be done in the autumn in order to allow winter settling, and the plantations will look more attractive if their new home bed is somewhat rumpled in its levels. A few well placed rocks of moderate size and well aged in surface will add to the informality and naturalness of the group.

The new plants should be set out in spring, and not planted too closely, as a group tightly huddled together gives the same feeling of oppression as a crowded small room. Copious watering should be done in dry periods, not skimpy sprinkles.

In winter the Reef Point heaths and heathers are pretty thoroughly covered with spruce boughs, to prevent stem splitting among the heaths and burning of foliage in the heathers. In spring the heathers are clipped, and if a superannuated and straggly plant is found, it is replaced by a younger one. Each spring a light dressing of ground peat should be tucked in around the bases of the plants to give added moisture holding quality to the soil over the roots.

There are many varieties of heathers, and the colours range from the single pure whites, through the pale lavenders to reddish purples and deep burning red. Their growth is as different as their colours, some cling to the ground so closely that the old plants look like a large bed of moss, others grow taller, to fifteen or eighteen inches, and carry their crowds of tiny flowers proudly at the end of stiff stems. Others are almost weeping in growth and make little mounds of pale pink or lavender flowers—and one or two are stiff and rigid in growth and spread horizontally rather than vertically.

Both heaths and heathers are among the most admired among the plantations, they take the stage in August and hold it until mid-September. The white heathers are cherished as bringing good luck and a safe return to the place whence they came. Those who live at Reef Point have often looked at little dried pieces of heather with smarting eyes. They have been carried to and from Guadalcanal and the grim heights of Korea. The recipients brought them back to their home. The growers had lumps in their throats and moist eyes when they saw the little battered twigs carefully wrapped upon their return from their long journeys.

> "The humming bees are still
> The fir climbs the heather
> The heather climbs the hill."

AMY MAGDALENE GARLAND

Calluna Species and Varieties Grown at Reef Point Gardens

Numbers refer to herbarium specimens in The Reference Library. Many have been identified at the Royal Botanic Garden, Edinburgh, Professor Sir William Wright Smith, Regius Keeper.

CALLUNA VULGARIS TYPE, blooming mid-August to end September. Plant height 15–18 inches, flowers on tips of upright branches.

608 CALLUNA VULGARIS ALBA RIGIDA, different in growing habit from other white heathers, angled stems, somewhat dwarf and spreading, flowers good but less full than in some other varieties. Useful for its difference in growth character. August.

1091 CALLUNA VULGARIS ALPORTII, one of the taller and upright growing varieties, deep crimson in late August, fading to deep russet in September. Plant very hairy and of distinct character.

1018 CALLUNA VULGARIS ATRORUBENS, somewhat like Alportii but not so deep in colour, flowering season late August.

1020 CALLUNA VULGARIS AUREA, leaves coppery in colour, and more remarkable than the flowers, plant dwarf, pinkish bloom in late August.

1007 CALLUNA VULGARIS COUNTY WICKLOW, a dwarf 8–10 inch spreading plant, blooming generously, shell pink double flowers, long lasting in bloom, late August to mid-September. A very good sort.

CALLUNA VULGARIS FL.PL. This sort is perhaps less good than H. E. Beale, but it has flowers of pale pink and good growth. August, September.

899 CALLUNA VULGARIS FOXII NANA, very dwarf, 3–4 inches high, flowers pale "heather" colour and not spectacular. Useful as an edging as it spills over stone borders and softens the plantation edges. August, September.

1002 CALLUNA VULGARIS J. H. HAMILTON, dwarf and spreading double flowers, pink in early August, stages of flower deepening in September to a warmer shade.

1015 CALLUNA VULGARIS HAMMONDII, a tall growing sturdy plant carrying its white flowers high and proudly, a well known and good variety blooming late August and well into September.

1004 CALLUNA VULGARIS H. E. BEALE, one of the very best of the varieties, flowers in long spikes, silvery pink double in tiny rosettes. Late in blooming and holding its flowers in good condition well into late September. Award of Merit given this variety by the Royal Horticultural Society.

940 CALLUNA VULGARIS KUPHALDTI, dwarf plant with twisted branches, distinct in type, pinkish lavender flowers. August, September.

CALLUNA VULGARIS MINIMA SMITH'S VARIETY, very ground hugging variety much like nana compacta, more valuable for foliage than flower.

1006 CALLUNA VULGARIS MRS. RONALD H. GRAY, a scrambling dwarf twiggy plant, not supposed to be quite as hardy as some varieties, but thrives at Reef Point. Flowers rather reddish in late August and September.

CALLUNA VULGARIS MULLION, low growing plant with deep pink flowers, perhaps a trifle less hardy than some varieties, August, September.

1017 CALLUNA VULGARIS PILOSA, a low growing plant with downy twigs, "heather coloured" flowers, blooming midseason August to early September.

1143 CALLUNA VULGARIS VAR. RUBRA, an early blooming low growing deep red sort, often confused with var. tenuis.

1142 CALLUNA VULGARIS SEARLEI, a good white variety, little bushes of neat form, single flowers in late season, September and into October.

737 CALLUNA VULGARIS TENUIS (identification questioned), earliest July blooming dwarf plant, free flowering, ruby red. Valuable for early bloom.

738 CALLUNA VULGARIS TIB, free flowering, double deep crimson flowers in long spikes, a fine variety. July, August.

The writers have been much helped
by Fred J. Chapple's book THE HEATHER GARDEN,
and wish to express their indebtedness.

THE REEF POINT GARDENS CORPORATION
Bar Harbor, Maine

OFFICERS
BEATRIX FARRAND, *President*
ROBERT WHITELEY PATTERSON, *Vice President*
ALBERT HALL CUNNINGHAM, *Treasurer*
ISABELLE MARSHALL STOVER, *Clerk*

Consultant
ROBERT WHITELEY PATTERSON

Horticulturist
AMY MAGDALENE GARLAND

Directors

ALBERT HALL CUNNINGHAM	LAWRENCE MORRIS
BEATRIX FARRAND	ROBERT WHITELEY PATTERSON
AMY MAGDALENE GARLAND	CHARLES KENNETH SAVAGE
AGNES MILLIKEN	EDWIN RAY SMITH

Members

ALBERT HALL CUNNINGHAM	LAWRENCE MORRIS
BEATRIX FARRAND	JOSEPH MAGEE MURRAY
AMY MAGDALENE GARLAND	ROBERT WHITELEY PATTERSON
FAY HYLAND	CHARLES KENNETH SAVAGE
SUSAN DELANO MCKELVEY	KARL SAX
AGNES MILLIKEN	EDWIN RAY SMITH
ROGER MILLIKEN	ISABELLE MARSHALL STOVER

ELIZABETH F. THORNDIKE

George Grady Press, New York

80

REEF POINT GARDENS BULLETIN

Copyright, 1954, by Reef Point Gardens Corporation

PUBLISHED BY THE MAX FARRAND MEMORIAL FUND

BAR HARBOR · MAINE

Vol. I, No 13   *AUGUST,* 1954   Price 10 cents

Sewall Brown, Photographer

A SIMPLE FOUNDATION PLANTING

Simple Foundation Planting in Eastern Coastal Maine

WHEN THE present horticulturist of Reef Point Gardens first came to Bar Harbor some thirty odd years ago, an unforgotten impression was made. After the sail across the bay on a late May morning the aspect of the village and its tidy houses was pleasant and friendly, but surprise was felt to notice how bare the grounds were and how scanty the flowers. In the south of England where the horticulturist's youth was spent, her neighbours, and in fact most Englishmen, took great pleasure in their gardens whether they were for the humble cabbage or whether they also had a little flowering plot. These cottage gardens have a charm all their own.

The northeastern American winters are severe and in many cases banking of the foundations must be made in order to keep as much as the cold out as may be possible, but in many instances there is room and in fact need for simple framing around the house and masking of over-high foundation walls or porch supports. Simple planting may be made with small expense and little upkeep is needed. There is great choice of material to suit varied tastes: for instance, a few wood ferns could be acquired, and among these the interrupted one (Osmunda Claytoniana) is the most graceful, interplanted zig-zag fashion with Daffodils. The daffys would be up and blooming before the fern fronds show above the ground, and by the time the bulb leaves are shabby and unsightly, the ferns will take over. This planting would be suitable on the shaded side of the house and would only need watering and a little weeding, and should stay presentable for nine or ten years, since Osmundas do not like to be disturbed.

As most village houses are free on all sides, opportunity is given for different treatments on each of the four exposures. On the south and east sides a Clematis or two would be pretty and as they are mercifully nearly free of insects, they are therefore easy to care for. Clematis Jackmannii is always striking in colour especially if it harmonizes with the colour of the house. Directly in front of this creeper Madonna Lilies make a pretty group, and are also useful as the Clematis tribe like their heads in the sun and feet in the shade, so the Lilies will shade the climbers' roots and keep them cool. Either a trellis or chicken wire may be attached to the house by hooks and if the wire is painted the same colour as the house it is hardly noticeable and the Clematis can then be trained up the wire, either by tying or pushing the young growth through the holes and up. Perennials would look well in this border and among these are Peonies in all their many lovely sorts, single and double, Iris of various kinds, Iberis sempervirens, the evergreen candytuft, Dictamnus gas plant, Dicentra bleeding heart, Veronica incana, Dianthus perennial Scotch pink, and any of the low-growing Campanulas, such as carpatica or garganica. All of these plants are good in height and the foliage will be presentable throughout the summer, with the exception of Dicentra which may get rather unsightly in mid-summer. However, this plant has the merit of blooming early at the end of May, and with a few tall tulips planted among the perennials and gaps filled with annuals in June, such as Phlox Drummondii, Petunias, Alyssum, Pansies, Lobelia, and any others, the border will be pretty throughout a long season, if the colours and size harmonize. If watered and weeded flowers in this three or four foot border will bloom from the middle of May until really frosty nights end the summer. If an edging consisting entirely of annuals is preferred a narrower one would look better, about twenty inches wide would be sufficient, but this implies a yearly planting and the bed would be bare in the early season unless bulbs are planted for early flowering.

Day-liles (Hemerocallis) Hostas and Pachysandra are of easy culture. These three might be called the lazy man's friends in a border. Nevertheless they have their uses and will grow where other plants will pout and sulk. Pachysandra is good on the shady side of the house and if a few evergreen ferns, such as Christmas (Polystichum acrostichoides) or shield ferns (Dryopteris marginalis) are planted with the Pachysandra they help to break the monotony as they give variety in texture and height to the bed. This planting will need only watering in dry weather, and when once established will not need dividing for many years.

Something must be said about an evergreen planting, since often one sees these beautiful shrubs jammed closely together and even squeezed in where they are far too tall. If Japanese yews are used, the low spreading sorts should be planted under the windows, spaced quite far apart, with the taller kind planted at the corners to give accent. Not many flowers would look well in this bed, but a few Snowdrops or other small spring flowering bulbs would fit in, planted in little groups in front of the evergreen with any of the white Lilies in between.

A few well selected shrubs are usually needed at the front door and corners for accent, these make a division and help to tie the borders around the house together. In choosing a few shrubs the Viburnum Carlesii would be excellent as it blooms in early June and is fragrant and the colour of the foliage is good in the autumn. Also the Rose-of-Sharon (Hibiscus syriacus) in its white variety is another good shrub; it has pretty shining bright green leaves and it starts to bloom in late August when other plants are looking weary. These two shrubs need little pruning as they grow slowly. Although most attractive, Forsythia is too often planted. This shrub makes much new wood each year and consequently needs heavy pruning after flowering, but not the kind it often gets, with its lovely head chopped off flat and waving side shoots trimmed to a military cut. Old growth which is always darkest in colour should be cut near the ground: this will thin the bush and give it air in the centre as well as keeping the new growth sprouting from the root.

A good evergreen shrub is Pieris floribunda as it will stand sun or shade, but it insists on an acid soil, it is neat in appearance and pretty in its glossy foliage and tiny lily-of-the-valley-like white flowers. There are many bush Roses, among these the Scotch Roses (Rosa spinossissima) are pretty and bloom freely in June, the foliage is fine and neat and the large hips add colour in the autumn; this Rose bush needs little pruning and no spraying as insects or diseases seem to let it grow without persecution. The hybrid Rugosa Roses are also invaluable and apparently invulnerable, they bloom throughout the season and are as clean as the Scotch Roses.

The house borders have been suggested but a small tree planted nearby, such as mountain ash (Sorbus), Laburnum, flowering crab (Malus) or flowering cherry (Prunus) will flower well, and the mountain ash and crab will provide food for the birds in winter, and a thorn (Crataegus) tree will also feed winter visitors. Any of these with a few well placed shrubs will give a feeling of privacy as well as make a screen to veil anything objectionable, or they will even serve as a background for a mixed border for those who may have sufficient space. Here the taller and bolder perennials might be grown; such as Delphinium, Phlox, Aconite, Astilbes of sorts, Siberian Iris and tall Campanulas, and many others. White flowers combined with grey foliage should not be omitted as these look cool and restful on a sweltering summer day.

In the perennial borders a little bone meal and a balanced fertilizer in early spring will fed and nourish the plants and keep them strong and healthy for a summer's display. These prescriptions do not need either a deep pocketbook or many hours of work, and they are easily filled by anyone who cares to make the house surroundings fit the ground and give beauty throughout the year.

One of the great leaders in gardening said "Plans should be made on the ground to fit the place, and not the place made to suit some plan out of a book." These words were written by William Robinson and are as true today as when they were written some fifty years ago.

AMY MAGDALENE GARLAND

NORTH SIDE: Ground carpet of Pachysandra terminalis or Hedera helix baltica, the hardiest form of English Ivy. In this carpet plant tufts or small groups of Christmas fern (Polystichum acrostichoides) and Shield Fern (Dryopteris marginalis).

EAST SIDE: A few sturdy perennials of good foliage. Easy ones are the Day Lilies (Hemerocallis) in their many new and lovely species and forms—flava, Thunbergii, etc., and the Plantain Lilies (Hosta Sieboldiana) Interplanted with Lilies, possibly the easily grown regales.

SOUTH SIDE: A Clematis, either chosen from the easy to grow species such as Viticella with small purple flowers or Vitalba with white flowers, or one of the many lovely hybrids such as Jackmannii with large purple blooms, or Comtesse de Bouchard, a lovely pinkish tint for late blooming, or the ever popular early flowering Nelly Moser, with big lavender flowers, striped with red. If Madonna Lilies (Lilium candidum) are not likely to be happy, L. regale will do equally well in height and colour. Among the Peonies that would enjoy the situation, the early flowering officinalis, the old fashioned "Piney" is lovely and has foliage as good as the albiflora types which flower a month later. Among these festiva maxima, a double white with a pretty red centre tuft is always good, and two excellent ones are Marie Crousse, a double pale coral pink, and M. Jules Elie a light pink and early. The singles are also good and are equally strong in growth. German Iris are as varied in colour as the rainbow after which they are named. So one may choose yellow, white, lavender, purple or smoky maroon. The dwarf sorts are also good in little clumps in the edging among the evergreen candytufts. Dictamnus, the gas plant, is not quite as easy a customer as the Peonies but is well worth a trial. Scotch pinks are attractive with their grey foliage and are apparently easy to grow. The bleeding heart (Dicentra spectabilis) is invaluable in early spring and if it grows sulky in midsummer a few tall growing snapdragons will cover its ill temper.

The annuals which may be added are as numerous as the stars—and one cannot go wrong with well chosen colours of Phlox Drummondii, Petunias, and the dark and light blue Lobelias and Alyssum.

WEST SIDE, OR SHADY CORNERS: If the west side of the house is open to the afternoon sun, perhaps a few small shrubs such as the smaller bush Roses, centifolia and damascena, and Deutzia gracilis will cover the foundations and not be too difficult to manage. In the real shade the interrupted fern (Osmunda Claytoniana) will thrive and early bulbs, such as Daffodils, Scilla nonscripta, (The English Bluebell) and some "smalls" like Scilla sibirica would give pleasure in early spring.

THE REEF POINT GARDENS CORPORATION

Bar Harbor, Maine

OFFICERS

BEATRIX FARRAND, *President*
ROBERT WHITELEY PATTERSON, *Vice President*
ALBERT HALL CUNNINGHAM, *Treasurer*
ISABELLE MARSHALL STOVER, *Clerk*

Consultant

ROBERT WHITELEY PATTERSON

Horticulturist

AMY MAGDALENE GARLAND

Directors

ALBERT HALL CUNNINGHAM	LAWRENCE MORRIS
BEATRIX FARRAND	ROBERT WHITELEY PATTERSON
AMY MAGDALENE GARLAND	CHARLES KENNETH SAVAGE
AGNES MILLIKEN	EDWIN RAY SMITH

Members

ALBERT HALL CUNNINGHAM	LAWRENCE MORRIS
BEATRIX FARRAND	JOSEPH MAGEE MURRAY
AMY MAGDALENE GARLAND	ROBERT WHITELEY PATTERSON
FAY HYLAND	CHARLES KENNETH SAVAGE
SUSAN DELANO MCKELVEY	KARL SAX
AGNES MILLIKEN	EDWIN RAY SMITH
ROGER MILLIKEN	ISABELLE MARSHALL STOVER

ELIZABETH F. THORNDIKE

George Grady Press, New York

REEF POINT GARDENS BULLETIN

Copyright, 1955, by Reef Point Gardens Corporation

PUBLISHED BY THE MAX FARRAND MEMORIAL FUND

BAR HARBOR · MAINE

Reprinted by courtesy from the Journal of the New York Botanical Garden

Vol. I, No. 14   *AUGUST,* 1955   Price 10 cents

Sewall Brown, Photographer

NORTH END OF RECEPTION ROOM

PORTRAIT OF LE NÔTRE SURROUNDED BY FRENCH GARDENS

Prints at Reef Point Gardens, Bar Harbor, Maine

"GALLIA est omnes divisa in partes tres" and this is true in a minor way of Reef Point Gardens. The part of the three which is best known is the gardening third, which is visited by several thousand plant lovers each year. The collection of plants numbers considerably over a thousand, and has been chosen with care in order to show what thin acid soil can happily produce in a somewhat austere climate. There are islands of less acid soil, where single roses, annuals and perennials and kitchen gardens are growing. Many plants are aliens but an effort has been made to blend these harmoniously into the native flora.

The living heart of the enterprise beats in the house with its reception room prints, and the springs which nourish the intellectual part of Reef Point rise in the Max Farrand library and the old book room in the second storey.

Linnaeus in court dress holding a spray of his favourite plant Linnea.

Many years ago when the present owner of Reef Point was a young student she tried to educate herself in the history of gardening and what the great garden artists of the past had achieved. In those far away days there was no course in landscape or architectural gardening, consequently many byways were followed which to-day's systematized education would omit. Inevitably drawn to the old gardens of Europe on account of the paucity of like achievements at home she was again baffled by the lack of photographs of great gardens, and as she was not an accomplished photographer herself she was once more inevitably led to searching for prints and monographs of well designed old gardens.

The result is seen in the reception room and libraries at Reef Point. Approximately one hundred and fifty prints hang on the walls of the various halls, passageways and rooms, and each has been chosen to teach some aspect of garden art, whether it be a clever adaptation of a design to a difficult and unsymmetrical site, or a grand series of terraces and fountains.

Marimont an unusual French topiary garden. Engraved by Israel Silvestre (1621–1691)

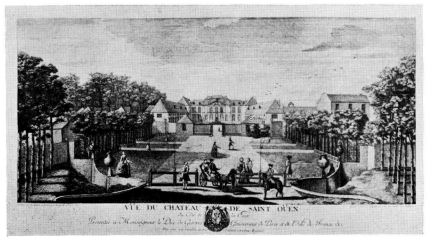

VUE DU CHATEAU DE SAINT OUEN

Entrance court of Chateau de St. Ouen. Engraved by Rigaud (1659–1743)

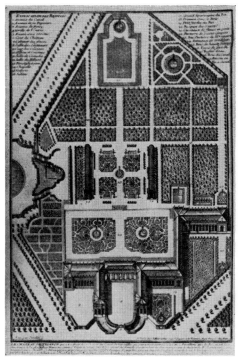

Each one is worthy of study, whether the strangely un-French topiary of the hedges of Marimont engraved by Israel Silvestre, or the group of great Italians from the plates of Pannini of Villa Conti, and the classic beauty of Villa Lante. The Villa d'Este is also represented in one of the most dramatic of Piranesi's plates. Many of the Italian prints hang in the entrance hall and French ones are added, many after Rigaud such as those of St. Ouen and Marli, and an Israel Silvestre group of various fountains and bosquets at Versailles.

In the large room especially arranged for meetings and conferences the prints are all of French gardens, presided over by Le Nôtre, where a stately portrait by Carle Marat hangs over the fireplace. The airy quality of space and light in

Le Grand Trianon. A formal design admirably fitted into an irregular site. Perelle engraver (b. 1595 to '98—d. 1675)

the Rigaud prints contrasts sharply with the more sombre pattern of the Silvestres—and as they each speak unmistakably of their period of Louis XIV or Louis XV they are interesting in their historic aspects of costumes, coaches, and general surroundings.

In the second storey room where the old books are cherished the prints suddenly change from predominantly French and Italian gardens to those of Brabant and Flanders. The grimmer buildings, the simpler, almost monastic gardens are strikingly different from those in the entrance hall and reception room. There are also some unusual pictures, a pastel by Odilon Redon, a red hibiscus in water colour by John La Farge, a Clematis Jouiniana painted at Reef Point by Sarah C. Sears, and an oil painting of lavender coloured poppies by Walter Gay, painted in Edith Wharton's garden at St. Brice-sous-Forét near Paris. There are dozens of the so-called "vues d'optique," not of great value artistically but entertaining in their range of subjects — Constantinople, Rome, Spain, Germany, France, Holland — all spread their bright colours in passages and alcoves. They may not be accurate as they were made to look as the engravers of the day thought they should.

In the Reference Library there are likenesses of Max Farrand, who used the room while he was writing some of his books, and who has given his name to the room. There are also portraits of gardeners — Gertrude Jekyll,

Charles Sprague Sargent, John Evelyn, William Robinson — and two prints of Linnaeus, one in court dress holding his favourite namesake Linnea, and one in the Lapland dress he wore when collecting in the North.

Each separate print or photograph has been chosen for its educational value. The reception room exhibits the variety of design in French gardens, the accents given by hedges, variation of levels, placing of buildings and the use of majestic flights of stairs or steps, the animation given by vases, statues and fountains. The earlier prints of the seventeenth and early eighteenth century tell the story of the pomp of court etiquette and of parties of be-wigged and brocade clad ladies and gentlemen of the King's court. The parterres "découpés" or "de broderie" and their variations show without words that the palaces or chateaux were occupied often in winter when design had to be marked by inanimate material, such as powdered brick dust, or different shades of gravel, relieved by neatly trimmed outlines in box and by punctuations of clipped yews rather than flower beds. It was as elaborate a world as can today be imagined and quite alien to our present way of life. Nevertheless there are ideas to be gleaned in almost every print, whether the placing and surrounding of a short flight of stairs, or the adapta-tion of a formal or semi-formal design to a plot of ground irregular in out-line and level. In the later prints of Rigaud, the solemnities and pomps of Silvestre and Perelle are simplified and made more elegant, but the details of the different French prints are full of ideas waiting to be translated to our day. It may be a mirror pool, or a fountain basin and its surrounding mould-ings, or again the skilled use of the science of perspective even in tiny town gardens, and everywhere there is a rich fertility of design and composition. The Italian prints in the hall almost invariably show consummate art in the use of water, whether gushing and spouting fountains or rippling cascades from basin to basin on a hillside near the villa. Sometimes a quiet pool in front of a grotto or in a parterre was designed as a reflector of sky and clouds. The gayety of the run-ning water and its refreshing sound of tinkles, gurgles and splashes makes a contrast to the sombre trees shadowing many a hillside and giving relief in the heat of an Italian midsummer day. The Ba-roque fantasy, sometimes carried to a point of the ridiculous, or tricks of "Giouchi d'acqua," as they were called in the contemporary prints are the points least commended at present. Guests were supposed to step unwarily on hidden springs which set in motion jets of water on the astonished and doubtless frequently indignant visitor.

Photograph of portrait of Miss Gertrude Jekyll by William Nicholson. Given to the National Portrait Gallery by her friend Sir Edwin Lutyens.

Villa Lante. Two casinos behind the fountain garden.
Designed by Vignola, engraved by Pannini. (1691–1764)

The quiet gardens depicted surrounding the manor houses and chateaux of Brabant are in abrupt contrast to the various phases of French and Italian garden design. The houses themselves show a more northern quality of reticence and aloofness and a desire for protection from a less gracious climate.

Again the total inaccuracy but gay colours of the "vues d'optiques" in the passageways depict scenes whether in India, Constantinople, Rome, Madrid, Paris or London with the same high heeled and hoop skirted ladies and brocade coated gentlemen. They cannot be regarded as trustworthy documents, but they do give a picture of a world as it appeared to the mind's eye of the draughtsmen of the period. The whole group of prints presents a history of western European gardening such as may more laboriously be gleaned from volumes of garden history which abound in the reference library.

The casual visitor may not appreciate the educational usefulness of the prints, but anyone interested in human life as revealed in its surrounding frame can trace the development and almost the daily habits of those who used and enjoyed the gardens some hundreds of years ago.

A small group of the gardeners and designers of recent years are gathered in the Max Farrand Library—a photograph of the elder Frederick Law Olmsted, designer with Calvert Vaux of Central Park in New York, and Charles Sprague Sargent who was the first director of the Arnold Arboretum, and designed much of its planting and so taught garden lovers to use many previously neglected native American plants. The British gardeners to whom we owe much of our knowledge and interest in grouping of herbaceous plants and hardy shrubs are represented by a photograph of a portrait of Miss Gertrude Jekyll by William Nicholson which shows the distinguished lady sitting in her room at Munstead Wood. This painting now is part of the National Portrait Gallery in London to which it was given by her friend, Sir E. Lutyens. The sensitive hands and thoughtful face show this leader of gardeners in her old age when sight was failing but not intelligence. There is also a photograph of William Robinson whose books—like those of his friend and contemporary, Miss Jekyll—awakened England to the long neglected beauty of hardy plants, rescued from cottage gardens where they had been pushed aside in the early nineteenth century passion for "carpet bedding."

No gardener can afford to overlook or neglect the study of these designers of the past, even the most modern and functional designing can be helped by reviewing the achievements of the old time, whether of centuries past or more recent years, since all good garden art must be founded on the basic principles of the study of the site, climate and fitness for its purpose.

The old saying is as true now as when it was first said or written:

"What would be fair, must first be fit."

August, 1955. BEATRIX FARRAND

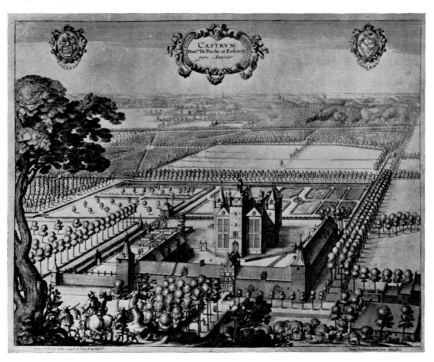

Chateau of Percke and Eelewijt. View of the approach and gardens.
Engraved by Lucas Vorsterman Junr. (1578–1640)

THE REEF POINT GARDENS CORPORATION

Bar Harbor, Maine

OFFICERS

BEATRIX FARRAND, *President*
ROBERT WHITELEY PATTERSON, *Vice President*
ALBERT HALL CUNNINGHAM, *Treasurer*
ISABELLE MARSHALL STOVER, *Clerk*

Consultant

ROBERT WHITELEY PATTERSON

Horticulturist

AMY MAGDALENE GARLAND

Directors

ALBERT HALL CUNNINGHAM	LAWRENCE MORRIS
BEATRIX FARRAND	ROBERT WHITELEY PATTERSON
AMY MAGDALENE GARLAND	CHARLES KENNETH SAVAGE
AGNES MILLIKEN	EDWIN RAY SMITH

Members

ALBERT HALL CUNNINGHAM	LAWRENCE MORRIS
BEATRIX FARRAND	JOSEPH MAGEE MURRAY
AMY MAGDALENE GARLAND	ROBERT WHITELEY PATTERSON
FAY HYLAND	CHARLES KENNETH SAVAGE
SUSAN DELANO MCKELVEY	KARL SAX
AGNES MILLIKEN	EDWIN RAY SMITH
ROGER MILLIKEN	ISABELLE MARSHALL STOVER

ELIZABETH F. THORNDIKE

George Grady Press, New York

REEF POINT GARDENS BULLETIN

PUBLISHED BY THE MAX FARRAND MEMORIAL FUND

BAR HARBOR · MAINE

Vol. I, No. 15	*JUNE,* 1956	Price 10 cents

SANGUINARIA CANADENSIS

(Bloodroot)

Native Maine Woodland Plants at Reef Point Gardens

During the year 1955 the Officers and Directors of Reef Point Gardens
and the Max Farrand Memorial Corporation decided that the two
enterprises should be ended, on account of uncertain conditions in the
future. The house has therefore been torn down, the gardens discontinued, and the library and other collections presented to the Department of Landscape Architecture at the University of California at
Berkeley. It is hoped that Mr. Beckett's two bulletins will be of
interest, but the plants which he describes can no longer be seen at
Reef Point.

PART I

LYING as it does in the great northern temperate forest zone, Maine is essentially a woodland state. So it follows naturally enough that many, indeed
the great majority, of the wild flowers are adapted for life among the trees.
Many of these have been cultivated in gardens for centuries, especially the
more showy and easily grown ones. Oddly enough it has been in the gardens
of England and Europe where many of these plants have found favour,
having been introduced by the pioneer plant collectors of early colonial days,
and not in the gardens of their homeland. This seems ever the way in coun-
tries that cultivate flowers for such is the keenness to get new plants from
overseas, that the native flora, with its often beautiful members, is entirely
overlooked. Indeed, it would not be out of place to quote the well known
saying: "A prophet hath honour save in his own country." For it can apply
equally to plants and men.

We live in a world of change, however, and of latter years it has been
interesting and gratifying to note a definite trend towards the real appreciation of native plants in the garden. There is certainly much in their favour;
especially since most of them, when established in suitable situations, are
perfectly trouble free and give beauty and interest throughout the years.

At Reef Point informality has been the theme. Many of the trees, mostly
red and white spruce and white pine, were left when the garden was laid out;
others, mainly deciduous species, have since been planted in suitable positions. In such a garden woodland plants can look their best, and feel at home;
use has been made of this fact.

In this bulletin some of the most attractive, and a number of the more
interesting and useful native woodland plants, either naturally growing or
introduced, will be mentioned. Light plays such an important part in plant
growth and nutrition that it has put serious limitations on woodland plant
life. This because for half of the year at least, the canopy of tree leaves blots
out most of the all important sunlight. This applies to the mixed, or wholly
deciduous woodlands, for few true flowering plants tolerate the dense shade
of pure evergreen conifer woods. To make full use of the sun, most of these
woodland dwellers bloom early in the year before the foliage canopy over-
head becomes too dense. Thus it is that the would-be cultivators of native

woodland flowers will find the spring and early summer months most interesting.

Cultivation presents little difficulty. If one is starting from scratch either in a small wooded area, or just under an odd tree or two in a part of the garden, the preparation will be the same. First, and quite obviously, clear the site of any less wanted shrubs, tree seedlings and weeds. Next, if the soil is shallow or poor, a good dressing of leaf mould or compost, well decayed, should be lightly forked into the surface. Never dig deeply, it rarely pays to invert woodland soil or disturb the larger tree roots. After the initial forking, all that will be needed is a little additional leaf mould as a mulch, either annually or biennially. Actual planting may be carried out in autumn, or in spring when the plants are just breaking into growth; exceptions to this rule will be mentioned later, but remember never to plant too deeply. If plants are gathered in the wild, try to replant at the same depth. If from a nursery-man, the following rough guide should be followed: plants with fleshy or tuberous roots should be planted fairly deeply, for instance trilliums should be planted between five to ten inches deep, depending on whether the soil is heavy clay or light and sandy in texture; but Canada Mayflower with a fibrous root system should be planted shallowly, about one inch, and never more than three inches. Many species will adjust themselves naturally providing they are not set too deep or shallow to start with. Young plants, and even old established ones, should never be allowed to dry out. If there are long periods of drought the soil must be given a thorough soaking when necessary, do not just dampen the surface, but make sure it penetrates down to the roots. Once the plants are happily established, little in the way of maintenance will be needed other than the occasional top dressings, waterings, and keeping a watchful eye open for wicked weeds.

An attempt will be made to walk through the season in the wooded parts of the gardens. According to whether the spring season is an early or late one, the middle to end of April will not be too early to start the journey. One of the first and loveliest harbingers of spring is, of course, the Bloodroot, Sanguinaria canadensis; from the time in early April, when the fat shoots thrust through the soil the plant holds one's interest, especially the quaint, lobed, crinkly leaves, each folded like a book, and sheltering the frail flower bud. A few warm days does the trick, and soon the whole clump is thickly spangled with glistening pure white flowers held just above the now expanding leaves. It is really worth making a pilgrimage to see such a clump, on a sunny day in April. However, this can be an exasperating plant, for it must have just the right condition to flourish, otherwise it sulks and finally disappears; in nature it grows on sunny well drained, lightly wooded slopes, in acid leaf mould, but even when we try to copy these conditions in the garden it is not always successful. A perfect example of this may be seen in the new part of the garden just south of the Atlantic Avenue entrance. Here a sunken

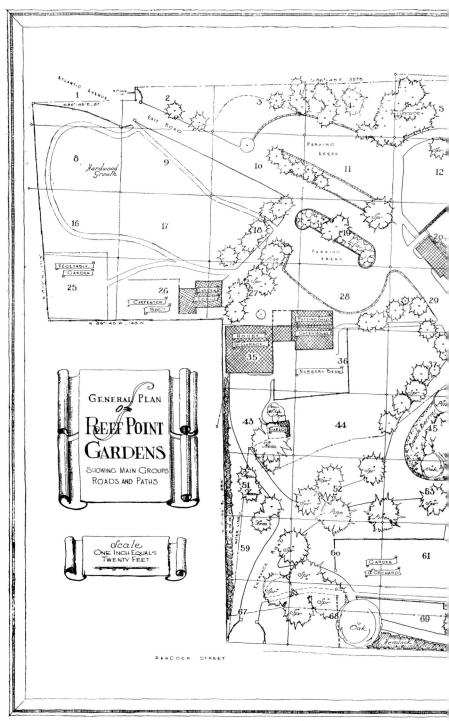

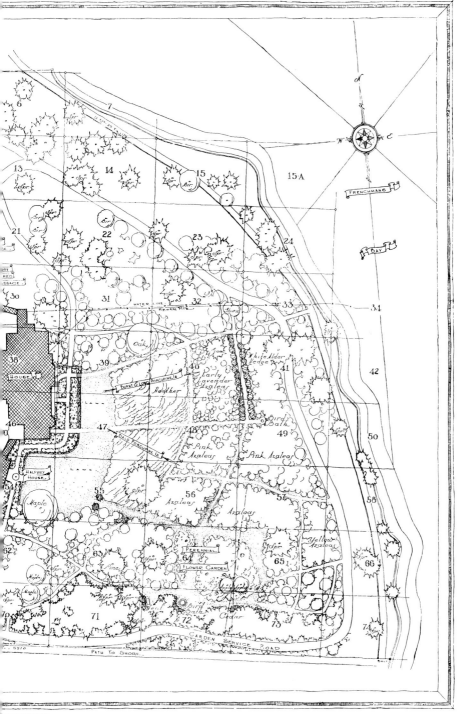

winding path running approximately north and south was planted with two groups of Bloodroot, one set out on the bank facing east, and the other facing west, the groups little more than a couple of yards apart. The sites were apparently identical, yet the west facing group has flourished exceedingly, and the other has all but disappeared. Perhaps the west aspect gets a little more sun, otherwise it is a mystery. A suggestion to bear in mind when transplanting, is to do it in late July or early August, while the leaves are still green, but make very sure the plants do not dry out, and also to plant the fleshy rhizomes shallowly.

Near this clump of Bloodroot are two more dainty little messengers of spring, each blooming about the same time. First the delicate and fragile but little familiar Spring Beauty, Claytonia virginica. This plant springs from a small woody, corm-like rootstock, and in early seasons is in flower before the middle of April, showing its delicate translucent white, flushed crimson pink, bells at a time when many other things are just awaking. Under the influence of warm sunshine, these bell-shaped blossoms soon expand to pink stars but the foliage is sparse, fleshy and grass-like.

Any shade of blue is always a rare colour in the early spring, and this makes the Liverwort, Hepatica americana, doubly welcome; once included under Anemone, but now placed in the genus Hepatica, the common Liverwort really includes two species, H. americana and H. acutiloba; however, they are much alike in flower and are therefore difficult to tell apart; bluish lavender is the usual colour, but variations are common and all shades from white through purples and pinks may be found in the wild. When the foliage is fully expanded in summer both species have handsome, glossy, lobed evergreen leaves. H. acutiloba, as its name suggests, has pointed lobes, and americana has rounded ones.

There is not much Rue Anemone, Anemonella thalictroides, left in the garden, and that is to be regretted as this is another little plant of the Anemone family of definite garden worth. Rarely more than six inches high, each flowering shoot consists of a smooth naked stem crowned by a cluster of lobed glaucous leaves and a sheaf of dainty, small white Anemone blooms. The creeping rootstock runs about quite freely when happily situated in a moist half shady spot, but is never a nuisance. This may be found south of the bog.

The May apple, Podophyllum peltatum, opens its umbrella leaves in the early season and lives in and loves the part shade of the hardwood grove near the bloodroot and hepaticas. Its wide open greenish white flowers and globular fruits endear the plant to many a child in woodland walks.

The American Wild Ginger, Asarum canadense, could hardly be called a showy plant even by wild plant seekers. Its woolly glaucous kidney-shaped leaves cuddle close to the ground and completely hide the dark maroon brown flower huddled close to the root. Its very modesty, however, makes it

Podophyllum Peltatum
(May-Apple)

noticeable on the walk leading through the woods to the south end of the perennial garden.

Then comes the Mayflower, Epigaea repens. This is surely one of the most welcome, and most sought after spring flowers. Really an evergreen, prostrate sub-shrub, this delightful little species is rather temperamental. However, given a cool shady spot that doesn't dry out readily in summer, it usually responds by giving abundant trusses of delicate pink and delicately fragrant blossoms.

Not all plants of the woodland floor are herbaceous. Indeed, quite a large percentage are sub-shrubby, or definitely shrubby. Not all are worthy or showy enough for a place in the garden, but a handful of species must be included. Either for flower, fruit, or autumn colour, or all three. The very earliest of these to bloom is the American Fly Honeysuckle, Lonicera canadensis. This is a rather straggly bush, that soon becomes clothed with tiny leaves and clusters of pendant Honeysuckle flowers as soon as the sun gains strength in the spring. Late April or early May usually sees it at its best. The flowers are usually described as being "Naples yellow," but in actual fact they are very variable, the best forms being orange yellow, the worst forms greenish yellow. They are followed by translucent red fruits.

A woodland shrub of value is the Hobble Bush, Viburnum alnifolium, with large hydrangea-like heads of bloom, each consisting of a flat cluster of tiny whitish perfect flowers, surrounded by inch wide pure white sterile ones. This shrub is an ideal subject where a plant for a shady site is wanted. Later, the tiny leaves expand, and may reach eight inches long by six wide; pale green and ovate in outline, they are both bold and handsome. In the fall near the Atlantic Avenue gate they turn a very striking, bright pinkish red, but the Hobble Bush is not an easy plant either to transplant or grow, it dislikes being moved and is not long lived.

KENNETH A. BECKETT

THE REEF POINT GARDENS CORPORATION
Bar Harbor, Maine

OFFICERS

BEATRIX FARRAND, *President*
ROBERT WHITELEY PATTERSON, *Vice President*
ALBERT HALL CUNNINGHAM, *Treasurer*
ISABELLE MARSHALL STOVER, *Clerk*

Directors

ALBERT HALL CUNNINGHAM	LAWRENCE MORRIS
BEATRIX FARRAND	ROBERT WHITELEY PATTERSON
AMY MAGDALENE GARLAND	CHARLES KENNETH SAVAGE
AGNES MILLIKEN	EDWIN RAY SMITH

Members

ALBERT HALL CUNNINGHAM	LAWRENCE MORRIS
BEATRIX FARRAND	JOSEPH MAGEE MURRAY
AMY MAGDALENE GARLAND	ROBERT WHITELEY PATTERSON
FAY HYLAND	CHARLES KENNETH SAVAGE
SUSAN DELANO MCKELVEY	KARL SAX
AGNES MILLIKEN	EDWIN RAY SMITH
ROGER MILLIKEN	ISABELLE MARSHALL STOVER
ELIZABETH F. THORNDIKE	

George Grady Press, New York

REEF POINT GARDENS BULLETIN

Copyright, 1956, by Reef Point Gardens Corporation

PUBLISHED BY THE MAX FARRAND MEMORIAL FUND
BAR HARBOR · MAINE

Vol. I, No. 16   *JUNE, 1956*   Price 10 cents

CORNUS CANADENSIS

(Bunchberry)

Native Maine Woodland Plants at Reef Point Gardens

During the year 1955 the Officers and Directors of Reef Point Gardens and the Max Farrand Memorial Corporation decided that the two enterprises should be ended, on account of uncertain conditions in the future. The house has therefore been torn down, the gardens discontinued, and the library and other collections presented to the Department of Landscape Architecture at the University of California at Berkeley. It is hoped that Mr. Beckett's two bulletins will be of interest, but the plants which he describes can no longer be seen at Reef Point.

PART II

MAY sees a noticeable increase in the numbers of species coming into bloom. Violets and Trilliums predominate. Once again, the new section of the garden, in the northwest corner near the Atlantic Avenue gate, will yield most species. Wake-robin, or Birthroot, is the first of the trilliums to bloom at Reef Point. This species, Trillium erectum, is not the most showy member of the genus, its three petaled maroon flowers merging with the shadows of the woodland floor, but there are lighter red forms and a striking white variety which are well worth looking for in the wild. Probably the finest of the New England Birthroots is Trillium grandiflorum, with robust stems up to eighteen inches high, surmounted by the typical cluster of three large ovate leaves, and crowned by a solitary pure white flower often as much as three inches across. There is a pale pink variety, and many forms, but none as good as the type. Flowering about the same time as the trilliums are the Bellworts, Uvularia species. The large flowered Bellwort, U. grandiflora, is the handsomest of the group, and a good clump can be a striking sight, with slender arching branches of ovate pale green leaves, and axillary borne bright yellow bells a-dangle. These are six petaled and one and one-half inches long; and similar, but with leaves that entirely clasp the stem, is U. perfoliata. A smaller version of the Bellworts is Oakesia, a dainty and demure little species, with flowers of buffish cream to corn yellow. No woodland garden or clump of trees would be complete without a clump of Dogtooth Violet. Maine supplies one of the best yellow flowered species, Erythronium americanum, also known as the Yellow Adders Tongue. This is a plant with handsome foliage and flowers: indeed, if the plant only produced its lanceolate, purplish mottled glossy leaves, it would still be well worth a place in the garden. However, almost without fail, it regularly adds the charm of golden pendant star flowers each spring, solitary, each on a slender arching stem, carried some six inches above the leaves (Sections 63 and 71). Goldthread, Coptis trifolia, must surely be known to all, with its tiny, dainty white anemone-like blossoms, glossy, lobed, trifoliate leaves, and bright golden slender rhizomes. It is an ideal carpeter for situations where the shade is not too dense, and soil conditions just moist enough. Belonging to the same Ranunculus family is Columbine, Aquilegia canadensis, everyone's favourite, as the airy panicles of scarlet and gold shuttlecocks are well set off by the blue grey, fern-like foliage. This is not a true woodland dweller, but is ideal for the glade, or near the edge, where a fair amount of sunshine can get through. And so to the Violets.

Viola papilionacea, the common violet of roadside and woodland edge with large purple flowers held nearly level with the leaves when the plant is in full bloom, is still one of the finest and most trouble free. White, and white purple veined forms are not uncommon. Another sort equally attractive, and by some accounted more so, is the Birds-foot Violet, V. pedata. Here, the very unviolet-like leaves are deeply incised and lobed, thus accounting for its common name. The flowers are paler in colour than in papilionacea, but held above the foliage throughout the blooming season (Section 67). The Canada Violet, V. canadensis, is very distinct, with leafy robust stems, and sweetly scented axillary flowers of purple and white with a yellow throat. Light shade and plenty of moisture are essential if this species is to do its best.

As May makes way for June, more and more plants come into bloom, as if in frantic haste to flower before the leafy canopy shuts out the sun. A small yet attractive Trillium, T. undulatum, known as the Painted Trillium, flowers now in the hardwood grove. Smaller than T. erectum in all its parts, the blossoms are white, each of the three narrow wavy-edged petals having a "V" shaped crimson mark at the base.

False Spikenard, Canada Mayflower, Solomons-seal and the already mentioned Trilliums, Dogtooth Violets and Bellworts, all belong to the lily family, or Liliaceae. This family probably produces a greater number of worth while ornamental woodland plants than any other single natural order. In the same hardwood grove False Spikenard, Smilacina racemosa, is happily situated in a moist, not too shady site, and is very attractive. Its slender, slightly arching stems, rising to two feet or more, are clothed with alternate ovate leaves terminating in a broadly pyramidal panicle of numerous tiny creamy white flowers. These flower clusters are reminiscent of many of the well known Spiraeas. Its charm does not end here, for after the blossoms

Mitchella Repens
(Partridge Berry)

small pea-shaped berries follow that change from yellowish green, spotted with brown-purple, through pinkish, and finally to translucent dull red. Solomons seal much re sembles the last species, but the top of the stem is more strongly arched, and the flowers are borne in the axils of the leaves of the arched top. There are a number of species of Solomons-seal, or Polygonatums. In P. canaliculatum the flowers are often borne in clusters of half a dozen, each individual bloom being nearly an inch long. As in all Solomons-seals they are white with pale bright green markings. These grow near the foot-gate to the Shore Path. Canada Mayflower, Maianthemum canadense, must be familiar to almost everyone, with its glossy lanceolate leaves and fluffy spikes of creamy flowers. The berries pass through a similar series of phases of those of the False Spikenard. This shallow rooted little species makes an ideal ground cover, gaining most of its sustenance from the surface layers of leaf-mould, and it will tolerate drier conditions than most plants. Bunchberry, Cornus canadensis, with its four leaves, four pure white bracts surrounding the flower-head, and cluster of bright red berries in late summer, requires little more in the way of description I feel sure. It is found in similar situations to Canada Mayflower, often in association, but prefers more sun. They are both attractive and useful ground covers. Bunchberry is at its best in midsummer with its brilliant berries carried proudly above the leaves. Neither of these two plants can be mentioned without Starflower, Trientalis borealis, for these three make a trio of indispensables for the woodland garden. Starflower is modest and pretty, and a worthy member of the plant family of great horticultural merit, the Primulaceae. In appearance it is quite unusual, for the sheaf of white star flowers spring from a whorl borne aloft on a short stem. The plant is spread by slender creeping rhizomes. The Bluebead or Corn-Lily, Clintonia borealis, must not be overlooked, for even if not conspicuously beautiful, it is certainly interesting. From a cluster of glossy, lanceolate oblong leaves, there arises a slender wiry stem topped by a number of small yellowish turkscap-lily like flowers. It is the fruits, however, that make one look again, they are an uncommon shade of Prussian blue, and often a half inch long; these fruits alone make it a species worthy of garden space. Another aristocrat among the low ground covers, and ranking close to Epigaea, is undoubtedly the dainty little Twin Flower, Linnaea borealis, var. americana, the great Linnaeus's favourite flower as he saw it in his native Sweden. This is another of the trailing sub-shrubs, and related to Honeysuckles and Viburnums. It is hard to believe this when looking at the tiny rounded leaves, and thread-like flowering stems, each carrying a pair of nodding deliciously scented bell-shaped blossoms in white and crimson pink.

Orchids seem to excite two conflicting opinions as to their beauty: either you like them or you don't, and there is usually no compromise. For those that do, mention must be made of two of the finest species that Maine and Reef Point has to offer. Both are Slipper Orchids, or Cypripediums. Showy Ladies Slipper is a very beautiful species, its botanical epithet of "reginae" being well deserved, for it is regal in carriage and beauty. A plant of wet woods, it must have a moist site to do its best. Under conditions entirely to its liking the leafy stem may be two feet high, topped with a large solitary white flower. The lip, or pouch, is of velvety appearance, and stained a lovely crimson magenta. The most plentiful and familiar Moccasin Flower, C. acaule, is quite distinct. In this species there are two basal leaves only, the flowering stem springing naked from between them; naked, that is, but for a single leafy bract which subtends the solitary flower. The pouch of this blossom is longer than in the preceding species and noticeably grooved along the upper surface, it is crimson pink in colour and but rarely white, the petals greenish, suffused with purplish brown. This orchid is more amenable than C. reginae, and will flourish under much drier conditions. Propagation is best effected by scattering the dust-like seed onto likely sites, and leaving the seed undisturbed. About five years will elapse before flowering-sized plants can be expected. Tiarella cordifolia, the lovely foam flower, likes a partly shaded rich soil, and from it throws spikes of creamy white tiny flowers in a simple raceme. Its flowers are at their best in late May and early June, but the cordate toothed leaves often turn to a beautiful red in the early autumn.

July brings us two beautiful little white flowered plants belonging to the

Shinleaf family, Pyrolaceae. First, Pipsissewa, or Princess Pine (Chimaphila umbellata). This plant is prized as it will grow in the deep shade of conifers, being normally found wild in stands of Pine, Spruce or Hemlock. The whorls of lanceolate leaves are dark shining green, and are handsome even without the added attraction of clusters of waxy cream or flesh coloured half inch wide flowers (Section 16). Commonest of the Pyrolas in Maine, and the only representative at Reef Point, is the Shinleaf, Pyrola elliptica. It is more a plant of woodland glades, but will tolerate fairly heavy shade; the leaves are rounded, and arise in tufts from a short creeping rootstock. The half inch wide, nodding waxy cream sweetly-scented flowers with an interesting long down curving stigma are borne on a naked stem in a loose spike formation. Toward midsummer the delicate and somewhat cantankerous Dalibarda repens, of the rose family, scrambles over the shaded moist rich soil, and opens its flat white and pinkish flowers close to the heart shaped pubescent leaves; it is literally a ground cover not over three or four inches high. It hugs the ground both with leaves and flowers. Another creeper, Oxalis montana, the American wood sorrel, makes a charming ground cover; its trifoliate pale green leaves are spangled in midsummer with whitey-pink wide open flowers, and where this plant is satisfied, it spreads fairly rapidly, but is never invasive. The midsummer woods in soft rich soil are sometimes sprinkled with flat little tufts of the Lesser Rattlesnake Plantain, Goodyera pubescens, an orchid which carries its small creamy white flowers in a spike, arising from a rosette of beautiful green leaves veined with white. This is not an easy customer to please.

There is no better evergreen carpeter for a shady or half-sunny spot, and none more accommodating and attractive, than the Checkerberry, Gaultheria procumbens; it is better known, no doubt, by its bright red, pea size, winter-green flavoured fruits. Nevertheless, the white waxy urn-shaped blossoms are well worth looking for amid the young glossy reddish green leaves during late May–June. Closely allied is the Creeping Snowberry, Chiogenes his-pidula. This little mat forming shrub, with crowded, interlacing thread-like stems, and thyme-like foliage, is more exacting, as it must have moisture and a spongy vegetable soil. Optimum conditions seem to be in sphagnum bog, in the deepest shade it can find, and here it luxuriates, and luckily all except shade are not essential. Acid leaf mould, and a shady site that does not dry right out in summer, usually keep it happy, if not as rampant as one would like it. The flowers, appearing in July and August, are tiny and greenish and generally insignificant, but when spangled with pure white, oval bead-like fruits, it can be a dainty sight (Section 62).

Last but not least, mention must be made of the Partridge-Berry, Mitchella repens. The dark green mats of interlacing stems and paired rounded leaves are handsome when spangled in the fall with numerous bright red fruits. And no prettier sight could be beheld than in June when these same mats are thickly sprinkled with a host of quaint and attractive twin tubular flowers in white to palest pink. Most amenable to cultivation, Partridge-Berry will flourish in the deepest shade of a conifer plantation, often being found in such situations in the wild. However, to do its best in flowering and fruiting it should be in half shade.

Thus ends a somewhat inadequate account of a few of the more attractive Maine woodland flowers growing at Reef Point Gardens. If it has in any way started an interest in and a desire to use the native flora, it will have served some useful purpose. But *do not rob* the wild by digging up roots of anything but the commonest species. Collect a little seed if you will, for this is quite the most interesting way of obtaining any plant. If the worst comes to the worst, seek your quarry from a nurseryman who specializes in such trade. Leave the wildlings for all to enjoy.

KENNETH A. BECKETT

THE REEF POINT GARDENS CORPORATION
Bar Harbor, Maine

George Grady Press, New York

REEF POINT GARDENS BULLETIN

PUBLISHED BY THE MAX FARRAND MEMORIAL FUND

BAR HARBOR • MAINE

Vol. 1, No. 17

BEATRIX FARRAND

1872 - 1959

BEATRIX CADWALADER JONES was born in New York on June 19, 1872, and her forbears came of Cornish, Dutch, English and Welsh stock. She became conscious of plants from her early childhood, as her grandmother took her into her rose garden at Newport, Rhode Island, and taught the child how to cut off dead flowers; and the four or five year old little girl trotted after her grandmother and learned many of the names of the lovely old roses of that day. Often in later years her friends heard her speak of Baroness Rothschild, Marie Van Houtte, and Bon Silène with retrospective enjoyment.

When she was eight years old her parents came to Bar Harbor, and she well remembered the building of Reef Point in 1883, the designing of the road curves and the cutting of vistas and first sketchy plantations. As she grew up into girlhood she naturally became more and more interested in plants, since she came of five generations of garden lovers.

A fortunate meeting with Mrs. Charles Sprague Sargent the gifted artist who made the drawings for her husband's collection of American woods in the American Museum of Natural History, changed the course of the young woman's life. Mrs. Sargent invited her to Holm Lea in Brookline where she met Professor Sargent, the first director of the Arnold Arboretum. Professor Sargent became interested in Beatrix Jones's love for plants and suggested that she study landscape gardening. He offered to throw the facilities of the Arboretum open to her, and for months she became the grateful guest of Mrs. Sargent and the hard working pupil of Professor Sargent at the Arboretum. One day he astounded his pupil by telling her he had a professional job for her. When she protested she was not ready, he smilingly answered that she must learn while working for clients. Accordingly she set out for her first professional work to do some tree thinning and remodel a little planting on a garden slope. Other work followed and as years passed she tried to heed Professor Sargent's advice to make the plan fit the ground and not twist the ground to fit a plan, and furthermore to study the tastes of the owner. He told her to look at great landscape paintings, to observe and analyze natural beauty, to travel widely in Europe and see all the gardens she could, and learn from all the great arts as all art is akin. Years of preparation were spent in accumulating such information as seemed likely to be of use, since there were no schools of landscape art in those bygone years. Italy, France, Germany, Holland, England and Scotland were visited and gardens studied.

When she returned home more work came to her and another chance meeting, with Mrs. Moses Taylor Pyne, eventually took her to Princeton in

1912 and the next year introduced her to University work which was to become a large part of her professional effort.

Quite early in her career the American Society of Landscape Architects was founded and although she repeatedly said in later years that she did not deserve the honour, she was made one of the charter members of the Association. As the years passed and her roll of clients grew she darted from Washington to Princeton, Yale, Bar Harbor, and Chicago wherever her work lay.

Another fortunate meeting led to a happy marriage with Max Farrand, who was at that time head of the history department at Yale. They were neither of them young and each had attained some distinction in their work, consequently they agreed to go ahead with their professional careers and the years of marriage enriched both their lives. When her husband was appointed Director of the Henry E. Huntington Library and Art Gallery Mrs. Farrand migrated to California, with many excursions to her eastern work and even to Devonshire. The summer holidays were spent at Reef Point, where the two Farrands worked over the garden, planned for the future, and eventually founded Reef Point Gardens, an independent self-perpetuating, educational and philanthropic corporation.

After Max Farrand's death in 1945, his widow dedicated her life toward carrying out the plans they had often discussed, and in his memory established the Max Farrand Memorial Fund to help in carrying out the work of Reef Point Gardens. With the unflagging and unfailing interest and help of those who surrounded her the house was completely remodelled, structural changes made, and the furnishing changed in some respects. The reference and old book libraries were installed and catalogued and the grounds altered for their hoped for use. In her old age Beatrix Farrand saw more and more clearly that changes which affected the whole world had bearing on the enterprise she and her husband had started. Careful study and consultation brought her to the difficult decision to transfer the Reef Point project to another setting. The library was manifestly the keystone of the plan and its use problematical in a place distant from other educational surroundings of like calibre. Therefore she felt her duty led her to make the material a part of a teaching institution where it would be used and cared for in a manner fitting its educational value. The library and related collections were given to the University of California at Berkeley for the Department of Landscape Architecture, where they were welcomed and at once made a valued addition to the curriculum.

As the permanent value of the Reef Point Gardens scheme lay in the library, the actual plantations became of less importance without the background of books and other assembled material. Consequently the gardens were discontinued and Reef Point as a plantation for teaching, came to an end, and Mrs. Farrand disposed of the acreage and her old home.

During her lifetime Mrs. Farrand received various honours which she greatly prized. The honorary degree of Master of Arts and rank of professor was given her when she was appointed consulting landscape gardener to Yale University. Smith College gave her an Honorary Doctorate of Letters, the American Institute of Architects made her an honorary member, and the Garden Club of America gave their Medal of Achievement. Later still The New York Botanical Garden gave their Distinguished Service Award, and the Massachusetts Horticultural Society their Large Gold Medal.

She felt her life had been a happy one, she was grateful for what it had given her. She was ever thankful for the affection and help of her friends and associates during her long life, and attributed much to having had the privilege of their guidance.

Lux perpetua luceat eis

FINIS

THIS IS THE LAST REEF POINT BULLETIN

IT WAS WRITTEN BY MRS. FARRAND IN 1956

THREE YEARS BEFORE HER DEATH

APPENDIX

Signs posted at the entrance to Reef Point Gardens
during the final years.

A view of the south facade and terraces around the main house at
Reef Point before the 1947 renovation. The porch and shingled turret are draped
in a variety of climbing plants Beatrix Farrand called her vertical gardens.

Opposite, a planting plan and plant list for Section A of the
perennial garden at Reef Point. For record-keeping purposes,
the drawings were scored into numbered sections.

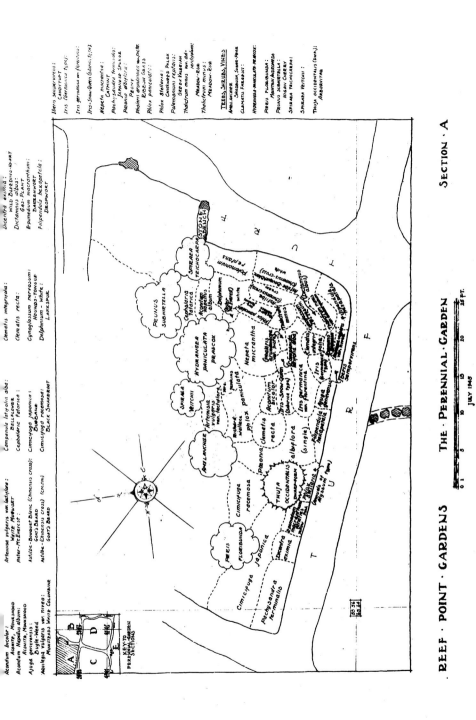

REEF · POINT · GARDENS   THE · PERENNIAL · GARDEN

SECTION · A

Robert Whitely Patterson, an architect and landscape architect,
worked closely with Beatrix Farrand and was vice-president of the Reef Point
Gardens Corporation. He purchased Reef Point from Mrs. Farrand in 1956.

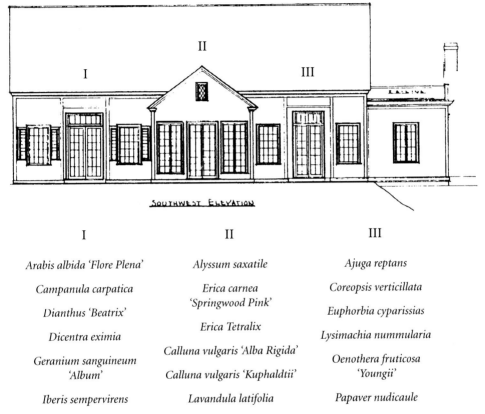

I	II	III
Arabis albida 'Flore Plena'	*Alyssum saxatile*	*Ajuga reptans*
Campanula carpatica	*Erica carnea 'Springwood Pink'*	*Coreopsis verticillata*
Dianthus 'Beatrix'	*Erica Tetralix*	*Euphorbia cyparissias*
Dicentra eximia	*Calluna vulgaris 'Alba Rigida'*	*Lysimachia nummularia*
Geranium sanguineum 'Album'	*Calluna vulgaris 'Kuphaldtii'*	*Oenothera fruticosa 'Youngii'*
Iberis sempervirens	*Lavandula latifolia*	*Papaver nudicaule*
Nepeta mussinii	*Thymus vulgaris*	*Polemonium reptans*

The southwest elevation of the Garland Farm cottage
designed by Robert W. Patterson for Beatrix Farrand in 1955.
Mrs. Farrand lived here after she left Reef Point. Each of the three rooms
at the back opened through French doors onto its own garden.
A partial plant list for each garden indicates those still in evidence.

Charles Kenneth Savage was the landscape designer
who created the Thuya and Asticou Azalea Gardens in Northeast Harbor, Maine,
as new settings for the Reef Point Gardens plant collection.

June 1, 1956

Mr. Charles K. Savage
Northeast Harbor, Maine

Dear Mr. Savage:

We shall all miss Reef Point Gardens
but when the future is dark, and the hope
we all had seems to have changed its
direction from east to the west coast,
we must tell ourselves that the new
future seems to carry out under new skies
the old hopes of the past. Thank you
most gratefully for all your interest,
your care and your friendship.

Yours ever sincerely,

Beatrix Farrand

It is a comfort to know
that the plants from R.P.
will continue their lives
with you —

June l, 1956, letter from Beatrix Farrand to Charles K. Savage
about the Asticou Azalea Garden.

Beatrix Farrand accumulated a collection of seed packets from around the world. A selection of these treasured seeds, still intact in envelopes, is listed here by source.

FRANCE

Vilmorin-Andrieux S. A. (founded 1775)
Producteurs de graines sélectionnées
4, Quai de la Mégisserie, Paris (1ᵉʳ)

Cobaea scandens
Dianthus (Chabaud selections)
Gaillardia grandiflora
Linaria cymbalaria
Myosotis alpestris 'Germinal'
Tropaeolum majus 'Nanum'

GREAT BRITAIN

Crown Estate Office
The Great Park
Windsor, Berkshire

Rhododendron pemakoense
(Accompanied by a letter dated
November 13, 1957, from the landscape
architect Sir Eric Humphrey Savill
commenting on the Forsythia x intermedia
'Beatrix Farrand' in the Royal Park.)

Royal Botanic Garden
Edinburgh

Gentiana andrewsii
Gentiana bisetea
Gentiana crassicaulis
Gentiana septemfida 'Latifolia'
Gentiana veitchiorum

Royal Horticultural Society Gardens
Wisley
Ripley, Surrey

Meconopsis betonicifolia
Rhododendron hippophaeoides
Rodgersia aesculifolia
Saxifraga 'Glasnevin Beauty'
Sorbus sargentiana 'Warleyensis'
Tiarella wherryi

KASHMIR

O. Polunin (1956)

Potentilla argyrophylla

POLAND

Hortus Botanicus
Universitatis Varsaviensis
Ogrod Botaniczny
Uniwersytetu Warszawskiego
Warszawa, A1 Ujazdowskie 4

Campanula alliariifolia
Dianthus superbus
Fragaria vesca var. leucocarpa
Lonicera tatarica
Papaver alpinum
Penstemon alpinus
Pyrola secunda
Primula elatior
Rosa rubrifolia
Thalictrum minus

SWEDEN

Hortus Botanicus Gotoburgensis

Clematis fusca var. violacea
Penstemon alpinus
Primula poissonii
Primula scandinavica

SWITZERLAND

Correvon Fils
Geneva

Aquilegia vulgaris 'Alba'
Campanula garganica
Geranium sanguineum 'Album'
Hyssopus officinalis 'Albus'
Hyssopus officinalis 'Ruber'

Acknowledgments

Publication of *The Bulletins of Reef Point Gardens* was made possible by the help and encouragement of many friends and associates devoted to Beatrix Farrand and the gardens she designed. A particular debt of gratitude is owed to Lynden B. Miller, who suggested the idea for this book, and to Patrick Chassé for his generosity in sharing his research. Others who offered either invaluable materials or their own expertise are Mary H. Barron, Kenneth A. Beckett, Jane Brown, Virginia Constantine, Diane Cousins, Maryhelen Davis, Eleanor Dwight, Virginia Dudley Eveland, Anne Milliken Franchetti, Dora Galitzki, Jerome I. Goff, Mary Ann Savage Habib, Julia B. Leisenring, Linda Lewis, Carl Little, Mr. and Mrs. Gerrish H. Milliken, Jr., Mr. and Mrs. Roger Milliken, Elizabeth Moore, Margaret Ober, Robert W. Patterson, Jr., Ann Rockefeller Roberts, David Rockefeller, Katharine Savage, Ellen Scott, Donald E. Smith, Judge Edwin R. Smith and Robert E. Suminsby.

Important archival assistance was provided by the following: Deborah Dyer, Bar Harbor Historical Society; Tania Martin and Jennifer Nardone, College of Environmental Design Documents Collection, University of California, Berkeley; William L. Mitchell, Landscape Horticulture Program, University of Maine, Orono; Laurie Whitehill, Rhode Island School of Design Library, Providence; Anke Voss-Hubbard, Rockefeller Archive Center, North Tarrytown, New York; Margery Sly, Smith College Library, Northampton, Massachusetts.

Appreciation is also expressed to Neva Goodwin, president of The Island Foundation, and to the many friends and supporters of the Asticou Azalea Garden and to its head gardener, Mary Roper, whose care of the garden would have given Beatrix Farrand great satisfaction.

INDEX

Page numbers of illustrations are given in *italics*.
Plants are listed by botanical name if it is given in the text, otherwise by common name.

Credits

A special note of appreciation to the following people and institutions who generously provided the archival material and photographs that have enriched this edition.

Cover, Beatrix Farrand's monogram: College of Environmental Design Documents Collection, University of California, Berkeley; endpapers, "General Plan of Reef Point Gardens," from *The Reef Point Gardens Bulletin*, Vol. 1, No. 6: Courtesy of Robert W. Patterson, Jr.; frontispiece: Courtesy of Mr. and Mrs. Roger Milliken; page xiii: Courtesy of Patrick Chassé; page xxiv, sketch of Reef Point gate: College of Environmental Design Documents Collection, University of California, Berkeley; page 117: Courtesy of Jerome I. Goff; pages 118 and 119: College of Environmental Design Documents Collection, University of California, Berkeley; page 120: Courtesy of Robert W. Patterson, Jr.; page 121, drawing: Courtesy of Jerome I. Goff; page 121, plant list: Courtesy of Virginia Constantine; page 122: Courtesy of the Thuya Garden; page 123: Courtesy of Mr. and Mrs. Gerrish H. Milliken, Jr.; page 124: Courtesy of Jerome I. Goff.